6/25/12

REBEL
PILGRIM

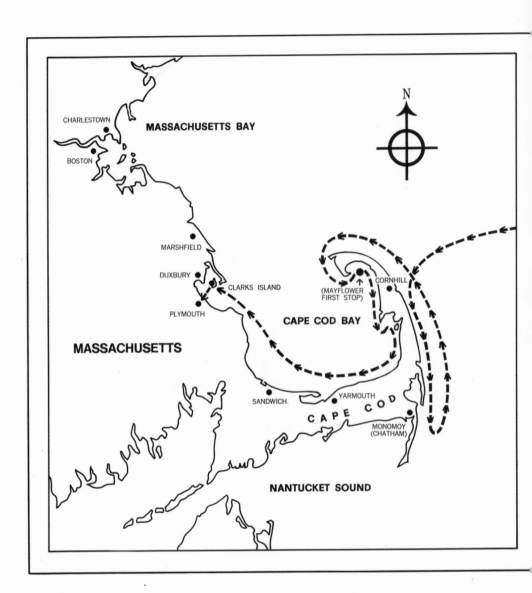

The route of those rebel Pilgrims

Rebel Pilgrim

A Biography of
Governor William Bradford

by

Wilma Pitchford Hays

The Westminster Press
Philadelphia

STANDARD BOOK No. 664-32430-4

LIBRARY OF CONGRESS CATALOG CARD No. 69-10387

PHOTOGRAPH AND ILLUSTRATION CREDITS:
Cape Cod Photos, Orleans, Mass.
Plimoth Plantation, Pilgrim Village, Mass.

PUBLISHED BY THE WESTMINSTER PRESS ®
PHILADELPHIA, PENNSYLVANIA

PRINTED IN THE UNITED STATES OF AMERICA

To
Susanna

CONTENTS

1   Secret Meetings   11

2   Escape   19

3   Twelve Years in Holland   26

4   The Pilgrims Find Cape Cod   37

5   Bradford Becomes Governor of Plymouth   46

6   Young Father of the Colony   52

7   Hunger   59

8   Bradford's Family   71

9   A Pilgrim Saddle on a Bay Horse   76

10 Plymouth Mourning for Her Children   83

    Afterwards   89

    The Author Says (including bibliography)   91

    Biography of Wilma Pitchford Hays   93

    Index   95

The first foundation or plantation is of more noble dignity and merit than all that followeth.

—Francis Bacon

Surely it was so with Plymouth whose influence has been beyond all proportion to its size. And at Plymouth the influence of Bradford is beyond reckoning.

—Bradford Smith

1

Secret Meetings

Young William Bradford walked between the ruts of the Great North Road which ran from Edinburgh to London. He met no travelers so early on this Lord's Day but he heard the bleat of sheep from an isolated farm and the call of wild fowl rising startled from their nests in the coarse marsh grass growing tall in the fenlands.

The countryside looked like a hiding place for Robin Hood's men when they had dashed out to rob a coach along this same road. William was not afraid, for no one knew—not even his uncles—that he was on his way to find the secret meeting place of a few families who had separated from the Church of England.

William had first heard of the Separatists from a friend who was herding his sheep near the Yorkshire farm where William lived with his uncles. Later, on several Sabbaths, the boys had walked eight miles to the village of Babworth in the next shire to hear the Puritan Pastor Clyfton, who preached "illuminate" sermons.

Among the people who had gone to Babworth to hear Pastor Clyfton were Master William Brewster and his wife and small son, from Scrooby, which was only about two miles from William's home. Several families nearby were beginning to hold their own meetings at Scrooby in order to avoid the long walk to Babworth, and also for a more important reason. William had overheard Master Brewster talking to his friends about this as they all walked home together.

Master Brewster said that there was a basic difference between the Puritans and the Separatists. Both were dissenters from the Anglican Church, but the Puritans wanted to remain in the church and purify it from within. The Separatists had withdrawn from the church in order to form their own congregations.

Now William climbed a small rise and saw the ancient manor house of Scrooby, surrounded by a moat and drawbridge, ahead beside the road. The back of his neck tingled at the risk he took if anyone knew why he was coming here, for it was dangerous to be a dissenter when Queen Elizabeth demanded that every Englishman attend the Anglican Church. State and church were one, and the queen could take the lives and property of anyone who questioned either.

What draws me to these Separatists in spite of danger? William thought. What makes me want to be with them? There were so many questions.

William knew that he had been baptized in the small Anglican church at Austerfield, Yorkshire, near the center of England in March 1590 when he was only a few days old. All the Bradfords still lived near this church and attended it. William's father had been a yeoman, a man who farmed his own land. His mother, Alice Hanson, was the daughter of a shopkeeper in the village, and he had a sister three years older than he.

His sister had told him that newborn lambs were bleating in their father's sheepfold when the family walked to the parish church where he was baptized and named for his father and his grandfather, William Bradford. Even now William felt a deep loss when he remembered these two. He had been told how pleased they were when a boy was born to Alice.

Then when William was a year old, his father died. When he was four, his mother married again and went to her new husband's home, leaving William with his grandfather Bradford. Before he was eight, his grandfather died. His mother took William again, but she died within a few months.

Again he moved, this time to live with his two uncles, Thomas and Robert Bradford. He had felt bewildered and lonely. His uncles were farmers and meant well when they began at once to teach him to herd sheep and plant grain so that, when he was older, he could take over the duties of the land his father had left to him.

The farm work was hard, and he missed the affection of his grandfather and family. Even his sister now lived with another relative. William became ill from loneliness. He often had to stay in bed several days at a time. But he had learned to read a little and sometimes he thought he was fortunate to be sick. It gave him time to teach himself to read well, and time to think. When he was twelve, he had read his grandfather's Geneva Bible again and again. He was so moved by the Scriptures that he wanted to understand more of their meaning. That was why he was on his way to Scrooby this morning to the secret meeting of the Separatists, who discussed the Bible freely at their services.

William crossed the narrow bridge over the swampy river Ryton and stopped at the gate of the moat surrounding the large estate belonging to the archbishops of York.

Master William Brewster was overseer of the ancient manor, as his father had been before him. Master Brewster was paid a salary to care for the forty-room manor house for the rare meetings held there by the bishops of York. It was also his duty to keep a tavern where those who passed along the Great North Road could stay overnight and eat. He kept fresh horses for hire and saw that the official royal mail was sent along speedily and safely.

It was whispered about town that Separatists' meetings were held in the Brewster living quarters in the ancient manor. William crossed the drawbridge over the moat, passed several houses used by families of the servants, passed the stables, the blacksmithy, the bakery, the brewhouse, and opened a heavy oak door into the tavern.

Coming in from the sunlight, William could scarcely see for a moment in the huge tavern room with its dark beamed ceiling.

Then in a far corner he saw ten or twelve men, women, and children seated around a heavy wood table. They were eating and laughing and talking together with the friendliness of a family group.

William had seen some of them at the services in Babworth and he longed to join them, but he hesitated. Would they recognize him? Was he welcome?

Master Brewster, at the head of the table, saw the boy and beckoned to him. "Come, eat with us," he called.

William came forward slowly, for he had no money and this was a public place where guests paid. A family on a long bench beside the table made room for William.

Master Brewster smiled at him. "You are welcome, boy. I remember you. Eat. There is no charge. It is my pleasure to provide for all our friends in faith."

"Thank you," William said. He was hungry after his morning walk and ate heartily. For no reason that he could name, he was happier than he had ever been before. Maybe it was because he liked cheerful Master Brewster at once, liked his kindness and his simple but learned manner of speaking.

William Brewster was twenty-three years older than young William Bradford. When Brewster was fifteen he had gone to Cambridge University, where he first heard of the reforms some learned men were trying to bring about in the Church of England. At seventeen Brewster had been hired to help Sir William Davison, one of Queen Elizabeth's diplomats. He lived five years near the court, where he saw and heard a great deal about the queen and the great men who came to her court—Sir Walter Raleigh, Sir Francis Drake, and others. He also knew of the dread Court of High Commission, which had sentenced one of Brewster's own Cambridge classmates to death for publishing a pamphlet about injustices in the church.

William Brewster had returned to Scrooby Manor as overseer when his father died, the very year that William Bradford was born in the neighboring village. Brewster could not help knowing the danger of holding meetings in his home, but his cheerful manner did not show any fear. When they had eaten, everyone went to the Brewster living room, where they sat for prayer and discussion of the Scriptures. Then they talked about their problems as Separatists.

As William listened, he felt at home. Here every man was allowed to speak if he had something important to say. These independent-thinking men wanted to probe the reasons for their acts and beliefs.

A yeoman, apparently new to the congregation, asked, "Why can't we remain Anglicans and ask protection from one of the conscientious bishops? Many good bishops, still in the church, have preached against the very wrongs for which we left it."

"Yes," Master Brewster answered, "but there are more bishops interested in gaining power and riches than in attending to the needs of the people. For years more important men than we are have questioned the injustices of the church. Without trial they have been thrown into stinking prisons, where they lay until they died of disease and starvation. Other leaders of reform have been burned at the stake or beheaded."

William's spine tingled. Was his faith strong enough? Could he endure if he faced such danger?

A burly farmer said, "Queen Bess is not such a devout church-woman herself."

Master Brewster nodded. "Queen Elizabeth reasoned that if men questioned the authority of the church, they might also question the authority of the crown, *her* authority. So she ordered that dissenters must be taught a lesson at once."

Young William was so interested that he could scarcely believe it was late afternoon when the meeting broke up, time for him to go home and help his uncles with the evening chores.

Master Brewster placed a hand on William's shoulder in a fatherly way. "We hope you will come again next Lord's Day," he said.

Mistress Mary Brewster gave him some seedcakes to eat on the way. The Brewsters' son, Jonathan, three years younger than William, and the baby, Patience, waved good-by.

Walking along the Great North Road toward his uncles' farm, William felt as though he were one of the Brewster family. Perhaps that was why he liked to be with the Separatists. They treated one another as members of one large family, sharing affection and food as well as beliefs. A strange and powerful happiness moved through William.

William's uncles and their families were waiting for him when he reached home. Even his sister was with the group before the fireplace in the big farm kitchen.

"You left the house early," one uncle said, "but you did not appear in the Bradford pew at the parish church."

William was silent.

"Where were you?" his uncle insisted.

William knew that he must confess, at last, his interest in the religion of the dissenters, no matter how shocked and angry his family was bound to be.

"I met with the Separatists," he said.

"You associate with these mad heretics?" his uncle shouted.

"Puritans!" his other uncle said scornfully, for the average Englishman lumped all dissenters under the hated name "Puritans." "Stay away from them or you will lose everything— your land and the good name the Bradford family has always enjoyed."

William tried to tell the family what the Separatists believed.

"Even many Anglican bishops think the church has lost its true love of God," he said. "We only want to return to the simple manner of living as set forth in the Bible.

"We believe," he went on, "that every congregation has the right to select its own pastor and officers by vote of the members. And every congregation should be independent, yet cooperate with other congregations in voluntary fellowship. We need no bishops, no archbishops, no central authority of any kind."

His family had been too horrified to interrupt. Now his sister wept.

"Such heresy will cost you your soul, Will!" she said.

"I must do what I believe is right," he said.

They sent him to bed without supper. But William determined that he would visit the Brewster home again and learn more of what the Separatists believed. Neither the wrath of his uncles nor the scorn of his neighbors, who made fun of all Puritans, could stop him.

When William Bradford was thirteen, Queen Elizabeth died and James VI of Scotland became James I of England. William stood with many other people beside the Great North Road as King James and his procession of attendants passed Scrooby Manor on the journey from Scotland to London. Everyone waved and cheered the king. The Separatists were particularly hopeful. They thought James, having grown up among the Scots, who had already brought about church reforms, would be more favorable to them than the queen had been.

Not long after the king was settled in the palace, a large group of dissenters petitioned him for changes in the church. One thousand clergy of England signed this petition.

King James called the Hampton Court Conference of 1604 to hear the petitioners. The more radical of the Puritans had caused all reformers to be unpopular among the people of "merrie England" by opposing games and feasting on the Sabbath. They had even condemned the traditional Maypole fun and jollity each spring on the village greens. So the four Puritan representatives were mocked and sneered at when they came before the court to speak. They were accused of being self-righteous men who wanted to spoil the pleasure of everyone else.

This did not help them when they were finally able to speak for the most important item of the petition, the right to freedom of conscience.

Before the Puritans could complete their request, the king flew into a rage. "I will have none of that," he cried. "Then Jack and Tom and Will and Dick shall meet and at their pleasure censure me, my council, and all our proceedings."

The dissenters had asked only for freedom of religion, but King James, like Elizabeth, saw that if men tasted religious freedom, they might want freedom in other areas of their lives, even in government.

"I will put down this Puritan devil even if it cost me my crown," James shouted. "I will make them conform, or I will harry them out of the land—or worse."

In the face of the king's threat, young William Bradford continued to meet with the Separatists at Scrooby Manor. And in 1606, when the people there formed their own congregation and elected Brewster ruling elder and young John Robinson as teacher, sixteen-year-old William Bradford listed himself a member, one of those whom King James had sworn to harry from the land.

2

Escape

The night was dark and quiet when William Bradford crossed the drawbridge at Scrooby Manor with a bundle of clothes over his shoulder. He hoped the Brewsters would invite him to stay with them, for he could no longer live at home.

After King James had ordered that every Englishman must attend the Anglican Church at least three Sabbaths in every month, William had continued to meet with the Separatists. His uncles warned him that they, too, could be thrown into prison if they harbored him.

One uncle had said, "Already Brewster has been charged with disobedience in the matters of religion, and brought before the Ecclesiastical Commissioners of the province of York. He got off with a warning. Next time you may be arrested with him, and that will disgrace us all."

William had said nothing. He had been as frightened as anyone when five members of the Scrooby congregation had been accused by the commission and given a warning. Master Brewster expected to be driven from the manor house soon. There was no longer any safety in England for those who wanted to worship according to their conscience.

"Fortunately," his uncle had continued, "you are not yet of age, so your property is in my hands and cannot be taken from you. But your life can be lost unless you come to your senses."

William was still shaken by the bitter parting from his family but he had made his decision. He would go with the Separatists. Where would they go? How could they escape? King James had said he would harry them from the land. But now the king had forbidden anyone to leave England without permission from the government, and he would not grant dissenters the right to go.

William entered the tavern and found men gathered around a table dimly lighted by two candles. There were about twenty men, some of them from neighboring congregations. Ruling Elder Brewster was again urging them to escape to Holland, a country that permitted religious freedom. Brewster had been in Holland when he worked for the diplomat Sir William Davison. And several congregations of Separatists had already managed to settle in Amsterdam.

"Our only hope is Holland," Brewster said now.

For a moment the men sat with bowed heads as if they were praying, so that William did not move across the room to join them until a man asked, "How shall we make a living for our children in a country that we know nothing about? We cannot speak the language. We are farmers, and I hear the Dutch live by trade and commerce."

"Then we must learn their language," another man cried, "and learn their trades too."

A third man stood up as if to go. "You can speak boldly, but I have an old mother and father here. My wife is not strong and cries at the thought of leaving her friends and the home we love so well. This desperate adventure to a strange land is a misery worse than death."

He left the room. Another man rose from the bench and followed him. But the remaining men were not dismayed and began to plan how they could get their families and goods from England to Holland without being captured.

William sat down on a bench as near as he could to Elder Brewster, who had become like a father to him. Elder Brewster described the latest plans he had made with leaders from the neighboring congregations of Separatists.

"We have hired an English ship with her captain," he said. "The captain demanded a great sum of money, saying that he must be paid well to risk transporting dissenters. But he has agreed to meet us on a certain day at a port we will name later. We must make ready, sell our lands and possessions as quietly as we can so we will not arouse the suspicions of officials."

Some weeks later William walked with a few families from Scrooby, down the road and across the moors toward the old town of Boston on the coast of Lincolnshire. Even the children walked the many miles, for the Separatists had sold their horses, since there was no room for animals on the ship they were to meet at the harbor of Boston.

William was almost grown now. He felt strong in body and in purpose as he walked beside John Robinson, the Separatists' assistant pastor and teacher. He admired young Pastor Robinson, who had attended Cambridge University but was always comfortable and sociable with all kinds of people and tolerant of other people's beliefs.

"We cannot expect everyone to believe as we do," John Robinson said. "We only want the freedom to live safely in our own religion."

William had never seen a town the size of Boston (England) with its old buildings and great church, whose tall tower could be seen from miles away. He was excited when he reached the docks and watched the sea for sign of the ship that the Separatists had hired to meet them here.

It was not in sight. The anxious people from Scrooby and neighboring congregations found rooms in the town and waited for the ship for several days. At last in the night one of the men, who had remained on watch at the dock, ran to wake the families. Men, women, and children climbed into small boats in the dark and were rowed to the ship.

They were scarcely on board when searchers, hidden on the ship, arrested them. The captain had accepted passage money from the Separatists, then betrayed them to the king's officers in the town.

The Separatists were carried back to the town. Their goods

were taken from them. Even the clothes they wore were searched for money. In the morning they were paraded through the streets. The citizens of Boston came out of their homes and shops to mock and shout and throw things at the prisoners. William was struck on the cheek by a rotting vegetable, but the sting of flesh was nothing compared to the sting of his humiliation. He looked straight ahead and tried not to show his anger and fear.

After a month in prison, the Separatists were released and told to return to their former homes. William went to Scrooby Manor with the Brewsters. A few Separatists gave up and said they would not try to leave England. Others planned all winter how they would try again to escape. Among those at Scrooby who were determined to go were Pastor Clyfton, who had left the Puritans to join the Separatists, John Robinson and his wife and little children, the Brewster family with a new baby girl whose name was Fear, and William Bradford.

In the spring, Brewster and leaders of neighboring congregations found a Dutch captain who agreed to transport them to Holland. This time they arranged to meet his ship on a certain shore far from any town. The Dutch captain told them not to fear, he would not betray them as the first captain had done.

A few days before the Dutch ship was to come, William helped load the women and children and their belongings onto a bark, a small sailing ship Brewster had hired to meet the larger Dutch ship some miles up the coast. The bark was too small to carry everyone, so the men walked all night across land to the meeting place on the coast.

William liked to walk and by morning was in the lead. He was first to see the ship waiting at sea beyond rough white breakers.

"It is here," he shouted to the men behind him.

His relief was short-lived, for he saw the bark carrying the women and children lying at low water in a creek that emptied into the sea nearby. The bark must have pulled into the creek for shelter while it waited for the Dutch ship. Now it could not move until the tide returned, a wait of several hours.

The Dutch captain knew the danger of discovery should his ship be sighted by a sheepherder or a traveler who might report it to the constables in the next town. He sent his small boat ashore with the first mate to urge the men to come aboard at once.

"Do not delay," the mate said. "If you men are on the ship, we can leave as soon as the bark brings the women and children."

The small boat could hold only half the men. Elder Brewster said he would not leave until the bark was free. William was among the men who remained with him.

"I'll be back for you as soon as I can," the mate said as he pulled away from shore.

The small boat had scarcely reached the ship when William saw the king's troops coming on horseback across the marshlands, waving guns and shouting.

"We are discovered," Brewster cried to the men remaining on shore. "Escape if you can, for you will be no help to your wives and children if you rot in prison."

Most of the men scattered into the tall grass and among the dunes. William and a few others stayed with Brewster to help the women and children, who were crying in fear as they saw the Dutch ship hoist sail and run to sea, taking away many of their husbands and fathers.

Brewster tried to comfort the weeping wives and children. "The captain had to leave or be captured with us," he said. "Trust God and have faith that we will join them later when this trial is past."

The troops arrived and took the captured Separatists into the town. Here even the constables did not know what to do with so many helpless women and children who had nothing to eat and no money. They were ordered to go home.

"We no longer have homes to go to," Brewster explained. "We have sold everything."

The constables wanted to be rid of the expense and care of so many people. Finally they told Brewster to take the families away—any place out of the town.

A few of the Separatists went home to relatives. Others managed to get food from sympathetic persons who were brave enough to risk letting the Separatists sleep in their barns and stables.

During the summer William helped Master Brewster arrange to get Separatists out of England one by one or a few at a time, since there was less chance of discovery if a man or a family traveled alone. In August (1608) the last of those who wanted to reach Holland were sent. Now William found passage for himself on a ship.

One day while William walked on deck, he saw a man watching him closely. Was he being recognized as a Separatist? Could he be arrested even now and returned to England and prison for being a fleeing dissenter?

When the ship docked at Middleburg, Holland, William was seized by Dutch officers. For a moment he was in despair. He was so close to joining his friends.

"What is your name?" a Dutch officer asked in English.

"William Bradford."

"That is not the name given to us," the officer said. "One of your fellow passengers reported that he recognized you as a fugitive. He says you are a felon escaped from an English prison."

This seemed too much to William, to be arrested as a common thief after he had escaped detection as a dissenter. He tried to control his anger and fear.

"I am English but I am no felon," he said. "I am William Bradford from a farm in Austerfield. I have friends in your country who know who I am."

As he spoke, his courage came back to him. He was only eighteen and might look like a youth to these officers, but he had endured many trials and conflicts to do what he believed to be right. With each difficult decision he had made and each responsibility he had met, he had come to feel and think and act more like a man than a boy.

The officer frowned and began to talk to his companion in their own language. William wished he knew what they were saying. Perhaps they sensed his strength and honesty and courage, for the first officer turned and spoke to William again.

"Our informer must have been mistaken," he said.

They released him, and William Bradford went on into Holland.

3

Twelve Years in Holland

William went at once to Amsterdam, where Separatists, who had left many parts of England ten years earlier, had formed a large congregation called the Ancient Brethren. He knew he would find there his neighbors from Scrooby and surrounding towns.

William had thought the old port of Boston was exciting, but he was overwhelmed by the city of Amsterdam built beside the Zuider Zee. He paid for passage on a small canalboat and rode up a main canal along the city wall. The boat turned into smaller canals crisscrossing the city. Finally William stepped from the boat onto a narrow main street.

The towers and gables of the tall buildings seemed like mountains looming above him. The people passing on the street were dressed in fashions strange to him, and he could not understand the language they spoke. This was a world so different from anything he had ever known that he was troubled. In this rich and bustling city, where could he find work? What could he do?

He soon learned that foreigners like himself must take the kind of jobs that paid the least. The Dutch lived by trade, and it took years to learn a good trade.

When William joined the Separatists, he found most of them working as apprentices to Dutch guild members. His friends were learning to weave cloth, or to be masons, carpenters, metal workers, or brewers. William became an apprentice to a Frenchman who had a reputation for making fine fustian, a twilled cloth of silk or cotton or linen.

William lived with the Brewster family in crowded rented rooms, and attended the church of the Ancient Brethren with them. Here he met Dorothy May, the pretty daughter of Elder Henry May. Dorothy and William liked each other at once and often talked together after the services.

The next spring when a few Separatists, led by Brewster, decided to leave Amsterdam for Leyden, William hated to leave Dorothy. She was much too young to think of marriage. William was not ready to marry either, but he told her that he would return to visit sometime.

Leyden was famous for hand-woven cloth, and the Separatists hoped to improve their living conditions there. William, with the Brewster and Robinson families, took passage on a boat. He watched as it entered the mouth of the river Rhine, then passed along canals through lush green meadows and finally between high spires of clean buildings within the city walls.

William thought Leyden the most beautiful city in the world. He marveled at the way in which the Dutch people had built a beautiful country from so little land. With dikes and water pumps they had turned patches of tideland into islands. These Dutch were not afraid of hard labor, yet they used their heads, too, planning and working together. If they could build such a country from land wrested from the sea, men should be able to build a country anywhere.

During the next few years William and his friends worked as hard as their Dutch neighbors, yet they had to live in such poor and crowded houses as they could find to rent. They worshiped in their homes or, as their numbers increased, in storehouses or wherever they could find a place.

Elder Brewster had used most of his own money to buy passage from England for those members of the Scrooby congregation who had been captured by the troops. Although William shared what little he was paid as a fustian weaver, he and the Brewsters scarcely had enough to eat until Elder Brewster was asked to teach English to some of the students at the University of Leyden.

William was learning to speak and understand Dutch from his fellow workers. He studied Latin and Greek, too, in his spare time. And he attended many lectures and debates at the university, for he liked to learn.

In 1611, the year that William was twenty-one and inherited a share of his father's land, the Separatists of Leyden pooled their money for a down payment on a large old house. This was the house where their pastor, John Robinson, lived and where they held their meetings. The house was known as the Groenepoort on the Kloosteeg, the Green Gate on Bell Alley. In its great walled garden, bordered by the Dark Canal, the congregation finally built twenty-one small houses for the families who had lost everything when they left England and who were still struggling to make a living.

William wanted to pay his share of the cost of the Green Gate house. He wrote to his family in England and asked them to sell his property there. It brought a fair price, for his nine and a half acres was good land with a house and garden on it.

Now William, who had always lived in someone else's home, bought a small house of his own on the Achtergracht or Back Canal. He chose it near the university and the meetinghouse, for he planned to marry and wanted his future family to be near school and church. He wanted to make the best living he could for them too, so he bought a loom for weaving fustian and set it up in his house to go into business for himself. Only a citizen of Holland could become a member of the powerful guilds that controlled business, so William Bradford became a Dutch citizen.

In December 1613, he went to Amsterdam and married sixteen-year-old Dorothy May, whom he had liked so much when he lived there. He brought her to live in Leyden. Two years later they had a son whom they named John after their good friend and pastor, John Robinson.

William and Dorothy were happy as a part of the large family of Separatists. They visited back and forth almost daily with the

Brewsters, Robinsons, Whites, and Fullers. And they met a new friend, a young printer, Edward Winslow.

Winslow had come over from London to work for Elder Brewster, who had recently set up a printing press in a part of his home. Brewster printed books and religious pamphlets that had been forbidden in England, since they attacked the injustices in the church there. The pamphlets were being smuggled to England and sold.

Edward Winslow was not a Separatist, but he was a man of learning and culture. William liked to talk with him, and Edward enjoyed eating supper with the young Bradford family. He often played with little John before Dorothy put the baby to bed. Then Edward and William, sipping from mugs of ale, sat before the fireplace and discussed many things.

"I'm impressed," Edward said one evening, "with the sincere affection of the Separatists for one another. You seem to be one big family."

"We who love God are all brothers," William said, "and should help and comfort one another."

"I admire the Hollanders too," Edward said. "They are tolerant of freedom in religion and government, and are thrifty. The Dutch have built beautiful cities and fleets of ships to trade all over the world. They have grown rich, yet they spend their money wisely on schools to educate their children, on hospitals, and on art and music."

William nodded. "The Hollanders have done all this in spite of having to fight Spain for years and years to keep their lands from being invaded," he said. "It is difficult to remember that every citizen of Leyden over forty years of age has lived through the siege by the Spaniards, who cut their dikes and let the sea ruin their land."

Both Edward and William knew that the Dutch of Leyden had gathered within the city walls and held out for months against their enemy. They ate every blade of grass, even rats and mice, and still they would not surrender to the Spaniards.

Eight thousand people in Leyden died of starvation. Yet those who still lived had sent a letter to the Spanish besiegers saying,

"When the last hour has come, with our own hands we will set fire to the city and perish—men, women, and children together —in the flames rather than suffer our liberties to be crushed."

At last a fleet of Dutch relief ships had come and driven the Spaniards away. The weeping people of Leyden had gone at once to their church to thank God. Even now, each fall, they held a day of thanksgiving for their deliverance.

"Could you Separatists suffer like that for your beliefs?" Edward asked.

William Bradford thought a moment. "We have had great trials," he said, "but they are as flea bitings compared to what Leyden's people suffered to escape the rule and religion of the Spaniards. Yet, we could do it. Yes, we could do it."

"Did you know," Edward asked, "that the truce which the Dutch signed with the Spaniards has only a few short years left to run?"

"Yes," William Bradford said. "On every street men talk of war. Our congregation is anxious, too, that the truce between the Dutch and the Spanish is almost at an end. Who knows whether they will fight again? And if they do, who will win? Freedom of religion would be lost to all if Spain should win."

Edward was silent, looking into the fire.

"Our congregation is concerned about other conditions here too," William said. "Our children go to Dutch schools and speak Dutch more and more, forgetting their former language. Even in exile, we want them to remain English.

"Many of our people must take jobs at heavy labor to make a living," he added. "They work far beyond their strength, especially our children and older people."

William stood up and walked to the fireplace and faced Edward. "Without land of our own," he said, "we will never have security. On the farm in England, we grew the food we ate. We need cattle and chickens and fields to grow grain. Until we own land again, most of us must endure poverty without hope. Yet land is so scarce in Holland, we cannot get it. We must find land in some other place."

"I know," Edward Winslow said. "I have seen you and William Brewster often enough studying that map John Smith made of the coastline from Virginia through New England."

William Bradford returned to his chair and leaned forward toward his friend. "America," he said, "*is* a land of promise. Don't you agree?"

"The colonists in Virginia have not found it so," Edward answered. "Only a few of them remain alive."

"But we will go as more than colonists for England," William said. "We will go as one large family who seeks a good life for one another. We will get away from the temptations and wars of the old world. Like pilgrims, we will begin a new kind of life in a new world. We will keep church and government separate and never allow the state to impose laws between us and God."

Edward seemed surprised. "You sound as though the congregation had already made a decision to go."

William Bradford smiled. "I *do* get excited when I think of such an adventure," he said. "To cross the ocean. To walk over vast lands and forests unpeopled except by a few savages. We are holding a meeting next week to talk about leaving Holland for America. Would you come too, Edward, if we decide to go?"

"I'd like to come to the meeting," Edward said.

Many men attended the meeting, for the Separatists had grown to a congregation of three hundred people. Elder Brewster sat with a half dozen other leaders on the front bench in the Green Gate meetinghouse. When he rose and explained the plan, William Bradford thought the proposition sounded so reasonable that everyone would agree. Yet men began to speak, from the floor, of their doubts and fears. Such a voyage to a new world would bring constant perils and dangers, they said.

"But the dangers are not desperate," Brewster answered. "Many things that we fear may never happen. And such perils as we do meet can be overcome by the help of God, and with fortitude and patience."

The men said that great sums of money would be needed for

a ship, and for supplies and necessities to begin life in a wilderness country where there was no place to buy anything.

"We have thought of that," Elder Brewster said. "If we vote to go, we will send two trusted men to England to borrow money from certain companies which were formed by men to invest in the new world, where they hope to make a profit from furs and gold."

Still many of the people were afraid.

Again Elder Brewster urged them to consider the value of what they might gain. "All great and honorable actions are accompanied by great difficulties," he said, "and must be both enterprised and overcome by answerable courage."

After many questions were raised and answered on both sides, the Separatists finally voted to leave Holland for America. The elders chose two trusted men to go to England to arrange for the voyage, Robert Cushman and John Carver. Both men were deacons and were acquainted with influential men in England. John Carver was one of the oldest of the congregation, about fifty, a well-to-do merchant who had been born near Scrooby and whose sister had married Pastor John Robinson.

After many delays and disappointments over a period of three years. Carver and Cushman at last secured a patent to settle in the new world. In February 1620, the written patent was sent to Holland so that the congregation might read it and agree to its terms. The Separatists, who were beginning to feel like pilgrims in their search for a new way of life, held a solemn meeting to seek the Lord's direction.

This time William Bradford was one of the leaders seated on the front bench of the Green Gate meetinghouse. How he wished that Elder Brewster were there. But the leader who had done so much to get the Separatists out of England and urged them to go to America was in hiding somewhere in England.

Elder Brewster had gone quietly and secretly to London to help with the negotiations for the patent. At the very time that he was there, the English government discovered that Brewster was the man who printed the pamphlet *Perth Assembly*, an attack on King James and his bishops for trying to force English religion upon the Scots. The English consul in Leyden had persuaded the Dutch officers to arrest Brewster. They had searched his home, never dreaming that he was in England where friends were hiding him.

That had been months ago. Nothing had been heard from Elder Brewster since. All the Pilgrims were anxious about him and missed his advice.

William Bradford was twenty-nine-years old, yet the Pilgrims trusted his judgment and courage, for he had been like a son to Brewster and had learned a great deal from the older man. He accepted Brewster's responsibility among the leaders and tried to make decisions that were best for the whole congregation.

The Separatists voted to accept the terms of the patent from the Virginia Company although many Pilgrims were against going to Virginia where, it was reported, the colonists were dying like flies from fever and hunger. Bradford was one of those who wanted to settle farther north on the coast in an area Captain John Smith had named "New England" on his map.

"For," William Bradford argued, "if we settle near the Anglicans already in Virginia, we would be as much persecuted for religion's sake as we were in England."

Without resolving this issue, the congregation turned to choosing the members who would go on the first voyage, for there would be room for less than half the congregation on the two ships they planned to take. They would pool their money and buy one ship to keep for their use in the new world. They would hire the other ship.

Pastor Robinson said that he would remain in Holland with the larger part of the congregation until they too could afford to go. The Pilgrims wanted Elder Brewster to go with them to America if he was still alive and could join them, as they prayed he was.

William Bradford and Edward Winslow, who had now joined the Separatist congregation, were eager to go. Both young men were taking their wives. Dorothy was so worried about the dangers of a wild faraway land that she finally decided to leave her little son with friends until the Pilgrims had made a safe settlement in America.

Bradford, as did other Pilgrims who were going, sold his house and belongings to buy supplies and clothing that he would need in the new land. They were ready to go when word reached them that investors in the Virginia Company had quarreled. The Company had split into two groups and was unable to raise the money to buy supplies and transportation for the Pilgrims, as it had promised to do.

William Bradford met with other leaders to discuss what they could do. The Pilgrims had some money, but not nearly enough to begin a colony in a wilderness. To their surprise, the Dutch New Netherlands Company offered passage and supplies to the Pilgrims if they would settle that part of America which the Dutch claimed. "For," a Dutch investor said, "we have found you to be honest, hardworking men with a purpose, the kind of people we want as colonists."

The Pilgrims appreciated this offer but refused it. Even as exiles, they were Englishmen and wanted to remain English.

While the Pilgrims were wondering what they could do now, a London merchant, Thomas Weston, came to them. He talked to the men in a meeting. He said that he and some of his friends were ready to "adventure" money. He would form a stock company and supply all the needs of the Pilgrims to go to America, if the Pilgrims would sign an agreement to share with the investors or adventurers half of all their profits in furs, land, fishing, or any undertaking until the money was repaid with interest.

"Make ready," Thomas Weston said in his persuasive manner, "and neither fear want of money nor shipping, for all will be provided."

Gladly the Pilgrims agreed and a set of conditions was drawn up and signed by four leaders, Bradford, Fuller, Winslow, and Allerton. But when Weston returned to London, he went to Robert Cushman, the Pilgrim representative there, and said his fellow Adventurers would not agree to the conditions signed in

Holland. He asked Cushman to sign other terms. If he did not, the Adventurers refused to invest their money. In desperation and without consulting the Pilgrims, Cushman signed the new terms. The contract was sent to Holland.

William Bradford was shocked when he received the new conditions. He handed the paper to Edward Winslow to read.

"We are little more than bond servants to the Adventurers," Bradford said. "For the life of this contract, seven years, no man can earn a penny for himself."

Edward Winslow studied the paper and agreed. "Each Adventurer who puts in ten pounds," he said, "will gain as much as a man who labors for seven years and risks his life in the wilderness."

Now many of the Pilgrims who had sold their homes and planned to go to America refused to go under these conditions. Bradford could not blame them, yet he did not give up the journey.

When so many Pilgrims dropped their plans, the London Adventurers began to look for persons in England who would go to America, men willing to go for the chance to gain land and to trade in furs. The investors felt they must send "strangers" with the Pilgrims or the colony would not be large enough to defend itself in the wilderness.

"We care not how they pray," Thomas Weston said, "so long as they work."

The Pilgrims, who had endured much to preserve their religious freedom, feared the addition of strangers to the colony. Finally they agreed, providing the Strangers knew from the start who was in charge of the voyage, namely, Bradford, Fuller, Carver, Winslow, Allerton, and Elder Brewster if he could manage to join them safely at the ship, as they hoped.

The ship *Mayflower* and her Captain Jones had been hired to meet them in Southampton, England. The Pilgrims also had been searching for a used ship that they could afford to buy and keep in the new world to trade up and down the coast with the Indians.

William Bradford was not impressed with the condition of the sixty-ton *Speedwell,* which he and some of the other leaders finally decided to buy. He had the ship overhauled and fitted with new sails and a larger mast.

The Pilgrims had planned to begin their voyage in the spring so that they could have homes built in America before winter. But by the time the *Speedwell* was repaired and supplies were gathered in Holland and in England, it was summer. Now, after three years of trouble and delay, forty-six Pilgrims from the Leyden congregation were packed and ready to depart for Southampton to join the *Mayflower* and begin their voyage.

For the last time all the congregation met together at the Green Gate meetinghouse to hear a sermon by their loved Pastor Robinson and to pray. The Separatists who were remaining held a great feast under the trees to say good-by to the Pilgrims.

The next day the Pilgrims boarded a canalboat and set sail for Delft Haven, twenty miles through canals to the port where the *Speedwell* was docked. Bradford had helped plan this voyage to new opportunity, yet when he saw his many friends lined along the canal waving and weeping, tears ran down his cheeks. He tried to comfort his young wife, for Dorothy had covered her eyes so that she could not see her small son struggle to free his hand from Pastor Robinson's and run after his father and mother.

As the canalboat carried the Pilgrims down the waters of the Vlietan and through river gates, William Bradford remembered the first time he had seen these lush green meadows of Holland. For twelve years this pleasant country had been his home. He must not be heartsick but must lift his eyes to heaven and re-member the good he had learned here. He walked along the deck, speaking to his friends, saying, "Let us lift our spirits and have hope, for the Lord, our God, will go with us whatever we must meet."

4

The Pilgrims
Find Cape Cod

William Bradford stood on the deck of the *Mayflower* and watched the bright, cold light of the stars reflected in the dark waters. After the two months of stormy seas since the ship had left England, William found the calm so peaceful that he could not sleep. The others of the 162 passengers, huddled together in their crowded quarters, seemed thankful for the chance to catch up on their rest. Even Captain Jones and his thirty seamen slept, except for the helmsman steering the *Mayflower*'s slow progress toward the new world.

Would we have come, William thought, if we had known the terrors and terrible difficulties ahead of us? The Pilgrims had scarcely left Holland on the *Speedwell* when it began to leak. The ship managed to reach England where it was repaired but failed again when they put to sea. The *Speedwell*, in which the Pilgrims had invested so large a part of their small funds and hoped to use for trading in the new world, had to be abandoned. And the *Speedwell* caused the Pilgrims a far greater loss than money, the loss of precious time which they needed to reach the new world to build homes before winter.

The Pilgrims had reloaded their goods and crowded onto the one hired ship, the *Mayflower*. On September 6, eight weeks behind schedule, they put to sea again for America.

For two months they had endured storms in which the creaking ship seemed about to break. They had often eaten food with their eyes averted so they could not see the maggots and grubs crawling in it. They had suffered disease and cold and the hostility of the crew, who taunted the Pilgrims at their morning services of prayer on deck.

Yet Bradford was thankful that the rough seamen knew their business. Under the orders of Captain Jones, they had brought the ship far enough that they expected sight of land any day.

William Bradford had other reasons to be thankful, too. Friends, who had been hiding Elder Brewster in England, had managed to smuggle him on board the *Mayflower* before she sailed. Their loved Elder was with the Pilgrims again. And among the eighty Strangers, whom Thomas Weston had recruited in England, were several men whom Bradford had come to trust.

William Bradford knew that the Pilgrims would need friends among the Strangers, who far outnumbered the adult Pilgrims. Bradford liked John Alden, a strong twenty-one-year-old blond cooper, who had been hired to keep tight the ship's barrels of water and beer.

And he trusted Miles Standish, a short, redheaded former captain in Queen Elizabeth's army. Standish had been hired to handle the defense of the colony. Although he was short-tempered, he kept discipline among the men and still got along with them.

Stephen Hopkins was a little headstrong, Bradford thought, but he was courageous and experienced, having visited the new world once before on a trading ship. Hopkins should make a good colonist, for he had brought his family to settle, a wife and three children, plus a fourth child born on the *Mayflower* and named Oceanus.

As the morning light of November 9 began to light the sky, William Bradford watched Captain Jones and his crew begin their daily tasks. John Clark, the mate, pointed to the water. Bradford saw the color line where the ocean changed from the dark blue of deep water to the sea-green of more shallow water, which meant that land was nearby. A sailor began to make soundings. Then the sun rose, and a sailor called from the look-out on the maintop, "Land ho, land ho."

People poured from below decks, men, women and children, weeping with joy. They fell on their knees and thanked God.

William Bradford went to Captain Jones, who was consulting the charts in his cabin. "We are near the great arm of land known as Cape Cod," the captain said.

William scarcely glanced at the map, for he had studied it many times. He made his way among the people to stand at the bow beside Elder Brewster. His heart filled with "a great hope and inward zeal."

"There," he said as the bow of the *Mayflower* pointed toward shore, "there is freedom of worship and free land."

Elder Brewster smiled, but he was deeply moved too. "You are a young man, William," he said. "You should live to see God's purpose in bringing us through such deep perils. Perhaps He means us to lay a good foundation here, to be stepping-stones for others who come after us to perform His great works."

Whatever His purpose, William thought, whatever the hardships ahead, I'm glad we came.

It was late in the day before William saw the high sandy cliffs of Cape Cod ahead (now Truro light). The next morning Captain Jones headed the *Mayflower* south along the backshore and came into such bars, breakers, and riptides (Chatham) that everyone clung to the rails and to one another and was sure the ship was lost.

William Bradford's respect for Captain Jones's seamanship increased when the captain battled the shoals all day and managed to put to sea safely to deeper water where the ship waited all night. In the morning on November 11, the *Mayflower* turned back to round the point of Cape Cod and anchor in the quieter waters of a harbor on Cape Cod Bay (Provincetown).

Before anyone could go ashore, the men gathered below to read and sign a paper they had asked Elder Brewster and

Stephen Hopkins to write. From the moment the *Mayflower* escaped the riptides and turned back to Cape Cod, the passengers had argued about where they would settle. Some of the Strangers from London believed their charter obliged them to settle near the Hudson River. Leaders among the Pilgrims believed it was best to stay where they were now.

"The chill winds of winter are already here," Elder Brewster told them. "We must build homes quickly or we will die."

William Bradford agreed with him.

Many Strangers and bonded servants were ready to revolt, saying that if they settled on land to which they had no right, they were no longer under the law of England or any law and each could set out for himself.

"Then," Elder Brewster said, "we will draw up our own compact of just and equal laws for the general good. Our government shall be by laws of our own consent."

All night long Brewster, representing the Pilgrims, and Hopkins, for the Strangers, worked on the few paragraphs which Elder Brewster now read to the assembled men. As William Bradford listened to the words of the Mayflower Compact, he realized that it allowed more freedom under law than any people had ever enjoyed before. The laws were based on the Separatists' democratic way in religion, the right of every member of the congregation to vote for the officers and laws that would govern them.

Gladly William Bradford took the quill pen and signed his name under that of John Carver, whom the Pilgrims now elected as their governor for one year.

At daylight every person was on deck to look at the land. Fathers and mothers lifted children to see the beach and trees across the blue water. Sailors shouted at passengers to get out of the way so they could let down the great anchor. William Bradford found his wife and brought her to the rail to see the fair land.

"Smell the juniper," he said. "Some of us will row ashore today and get wood. We'll have a hot meal at last."

Dorothy, young and frail, barely glanced at the land. She turned and looked over the waters behind them and shivered. "So many, many miles from John," she said. "William, will we ever see our little son again?"

He pressed her hand but made no promises. He knew they must live in danger in this wild land. But for him this life also promised excitement and adventure and the opportunity to walk freely with God.

"You are sick of the ship's smells and of the sea," he said to comfort her. "After the Sabbath tomorrow, we will all go ashore. You can bathe and wash your clothes. You'll feel better when you are clean again."

He saw in her eyes that nothing would help her terrible homesickness and he did not know what to do for her.

William Bradford was so eager to explore that he volunteered for every trip to the land. The Pilgrims had brought a shallop, a fair-sized sailboat, but it had to be shipped in four parts and would take many days to reassemble and mend. They borrowed a ship's boat and rowed ashore on their first discovery.

Captain Standish led the sixteen men, each dressed in corselet with musket and sword, for they did not know what they might come upon in this wilderness of wild beasts and wild men. They had studied Captain John Smith's map, made seven years earlier, and read his enthusiastic description of the New England coast. Bradford, trudging through the soft sand, thought Smith was either overoptimistic or else he had not visited Cape Cod on a wintry November day.

The Pilgrim men walked about a mile along the beach when they saw five or six red men and a dog coming toward them. Indians. The Pilgrims waved, wanting to ask them where they could find fresh water and, perhaps, trade with them for food. But the Indians and their dog ran away.

Bradford and some of the men hurried after the Indians, but they soon lost their way in the thicket and tore their clothes, so they returned to the others.

The men came to a tree where a bough had been bent down

to form a bow, and acorns were spread around on the ground beneath. Stephen Hopkins held out an arm and cautioned the men. "Stay back. The Indians made this pretty device to trap deer."

William Bradford wanted to see the device for himself and came closer to investigate. The red men had woven a noose as cleverly as any English rope, he thought. He bent forward to see how it was fastened to the bough. The noose jerked and caught William by the leg and lifted him to dangle until his laughing friends cut him down.

Finally the men came upon a spring of fresh water. They caught up handfuls to drink and were pleased to find the water sweet and good.

From the spring near the ocean or back side of the Cape, the men crossed the narrow land to the bay side. They passed a fresh-water pond and saw a little river and came upon Indian fields with old cornstalks. They passed Indian graves and found a rusty iron kettle that must have come from some ship that had traded here.

They climbed a long hill and found where someone had smoothed a heap of sand. They dug and found a small woven basket filled with grains of corn.

Bradford dipped into it and held some of the blue, red, and yellow kernels in his hand. Such large grains, bigger than any grains he had seen on the farm in England. He hoped there was more of this, for the Pilgrims were hungry. How delighted the women and children would be if the men returned to the *Mayflower* with such food.

The men dug deeper and came upon a fine big basket with thirty-six ears of corn. Hopkins said, "The Indians store their harvest in this manner."

Smiling, the men gathered the ears in their hands.

Elder Brewster said, "This corn must belong to the Indians we saw."

The men stopped digging but they did not put down the corn they held.

William Bradford was troubled. In their hands the men held life itself, for corn was the crop that grew best in this country. If the Pilgrims survived the winter ahead, they must have corn seed to plant in the spring or else face possible starvation. What was the right thing to do? What was best for the good of the colony?

"If we take the corn," he said, "we must find the Indians who own it. We brought trading goods with us. We will pay them what they want for the corn."

Cheerfully now the men left Cornhill carrying some of the kernels and ears back to the *Mayflower*. More than a week later when the shallop was mended, thirty-three men sailed it to Cornhill for more Indian corn. They looked for the Indians along the way but saw no one.

Some of the men suggested settling at Cornhill. Snow had come, they argued, and the ground was freezing. They must hurry if they were to build homes before the *Mayflower* returned to England. Already the sailors were angry at the delay and had threatened to put the Pilgrims ashore and leave them. But Captain Jones promised to stay until the Pilgrims found a place to live.

"Supplies and water would have to be carried up this long hill," Bradford pointed out. "Surely we can find a more suitable place to live."

Most of the men agreed with him.

Finally on December 6 an expedition of ten leading men with several seamen sailed the shallop along the coast of Cape Cod, hunting for a homesite. Toward evening Bradford, huddled in the bow with his clothes frozen stiff from sea spray, saw on the beach ahead, ten or twelve Indians cutting up a great blackfish. They ran when the shallop headed for shore.

The Pilgrims made camp here (Eastham) within a barricade of tree boughs. While one man remained on guard, the others slept around a campfire, but no one bothered them.

In the morning the men laid their muskets on the beach to be loaded on the shallop. They were eating breakfast when they heard a yell like nothing they had ever heard before, *"Woach! Woach! Ha! Ha! Hach! Woach!"*

Miles Standish fired at the sound, and arrows flew in return at the Pilgrims, but no one was hurt. They caught a glimpse of the Indians running away.

After their first encounter with the Indians, the Pilgrims sailed farther along the coast, watching the countryside. The mate, Clark, and the pilot, Robert Coppin, talked about a good harbor they had once seen. It was around the curve of the bay. The Pilgrims had heard of this harbor, for Captain John Smith had marked it on his map and named it Plymouth. They agreed to visit it.

As they drew near Plymouth, a storm of rain and snow drove them toward shore. The shallop lost her rudder and the men struggled to steer with oars. They raised sail, and one of the masts broke. The men were half frozen as the little ship tossed in the heavy sea. Somehow they managed to get into the shelter of a small island offshore and to strike flint until they built a fire from soggy wood. Here they rested all the next day, for it was the Sabbath.

On Monday they sounded the harbor and found water deep enough to allow ships to come and go. "Deep water is good and necessary," Governor Carver said, "for us to trade up and down the coast."

They went on land and saw a brook. "Fresh water right by the sea," Bradford said. "And there are fields with rotting cornstalks several years old. The Indians must have abandoned Plymouth."

Then men looked around but there was no sign that Indians had lived here recently.

"We could use these cleared fields to plant corn in the spring," William Bradford said. "Surely God has brought us to this place."

"There are tall trees for building," Stephen Hopkins said.

"And a little hill where we can place a cannon for defense," Captain Standish added.

The men agreed that Plymouth was the best place they had seen to build their homes. They sailed on the shallop to tell the good news to their families on the *Mayflower*. Dorothy will not be so fearful and homesick when we have a home again, William Bradford thought.

When he climbed the ship's ladder onto the deck of the *Mayflower*, he saw strange pity on the faces of the friends who greeted him. Dorothy was dead, they said. She had fallen overboard and drowned.

He could not believe it, then he knew it was true. He could talk to no one but went alone to the bow and stared across the water toward England, as Dorothy had done.

How had it happened? Why? She was only twenty-three years old and so homesick for her small son. Pray God, he thought in his grief, that it was an accident.

5

Bradford Becomes
Governor of Plymouth

William Bradford leaned on his hoe to rest and wiped his forehead with the back of his arm. In the fields around him men, women, and children were planting corn, as the Indian Squanto had taught them. Five or six red, blue, and yellow kernels in a hill fertilized by three herring placed with heads together like spokes in a wheel. Even Governor Carver, fifty-five years old and previously accustomed to servants to do the hard work, was hoeing under the hot sun, for there were few Pilgrims left to work.

The colony of Plymouth was little more than three months old, yet half its people had died. All during the terrible winter, Bradford had helped tend the sick who were lying on mats of salt grass on the floor of the common house. His scurvy-ridden, feverish friends lay so close together that he could scarcely move among them. He had helped bury the dead at night and smooth over their graves, so that Indians watching from the forest might not know how few Pilgrims were left to defend themselves against attack.

Finally William Bradford had become ill with the fever and almost died. He remembered how tenderly Elder Brewster and Miles Standish had continued to care for him and all the sick people, lifting their heads to feed them broth, sponging their cracked lips, covering them against the cold.

God must still have work for me to do, Bradford thought, for

I lived. Only five wives and mothers survived, but most of the children lived. By age a very young colony, half of it children now.

Many of the seamen on the *Mayflower* had died too, for Captain Jones had not returned to England until a few days before. He had remained so that the Pilgrim women and children could live on the ship until the men were able to build a few houses.

William Bradford looked out toward Plymouth Harbor. How lonely it seemed without the old ship lying at anchor there. Captain Jones had offered free passage to anyone wishing to return to England with him, but not a Pilgrim left. Yet they all had wept when they watched the *Mayflower* sail for home. They were really alone now in a strange land. Their friends and families in England and Holland could not know whether they lived or died until another ship chose to visit this shore.

William hoed across the field and back, then rested again. How hot the sun was today, but the corn must be planted. He remembered that the Pilgrims had never been able to meet the Indians to whom the seed corn belonged.

Fortunately they had at last met other Indians and made friends with them. All winter the Pilgrims had seen signs of Indians in the woods, but they could never see or approach them. Like the Indians on Cape Cod, the Plymouth Indians avoided the newcomers. Then, late in March, an Indian had walked boldly into the village and said in English, "Welcome." He was Samoset, an Indian chief visiting from his home on a Maine island.

After a short stay, Samoset had gone away and returned with several other Indians. Among them was Squanto, who also spoke some English. Squanto had been captured here six years earlier by the captain of a trading ship who took the young Indian to Spain and sold him for a slave. Squanto had escaped and managed to get to England, where a sympathetic sea captain, making a trading voyage to America, returned Squanto to his old home at Plymouth.

He found that his whole tribe of Pawtuxets had died of a

plague, leaving Plymouth deserted, as the Pilgrims found it later. Squanto had gone, then, to live with the Wampanoags, the strongest tribe in the area.

The Pilgrims asked Squanto to carry gifts to the chief of the Wampanoags and invite him to visit Plymouth. They sent a pair of knives, a copper chair with a jewel in it, a pot of "strong water," and some of the last of the precious butter they had brought in brine from Holland. Chief Massasoit refused to come unless the Pilgrims first sent a hostage. Edward Winslow went to the Indian village and remained while Chief Massasoit and sixty of his tall strong braves crossed Town Brook.

William Bradford would never forget the tension of that first meeting with the Big Chief who was sachem over many tribes including those on Cape Cod. Massasoit had waited with great dignity until Captain Standish with six musketeers met him and his men at the brook. They brought the chief to a newly built house and seated him on several pillows on a green rug. Then Governor Carver came, dressed in his magistrate's purple robe to show honor to the chief. With him were the leaders of Plymouth, followed by men bearing drum and trumpet, and then more musketeers.

Bradford had watched the chief's face closely. Would he realize how few Pilgrims there were? How easily the Indians could destroy this small colony if they chose?

Governor Carver called for food and drink. When the Indians and Pilgrims had eaten together, their leaders began to talk of peace. They agreed not to war against each other, and to help each other if any outsider made war upon either of them.

Massasoit had been so straightforward and friendly that Bradford felt the Pilgrims could trust him. When the chief and his men returned to their village, Squanto remained in Plymouth. Filled with importance as the go-between for the treaty meeting, Squanto attached himself to William Bradford, to whom he had taken a liking.

What would we do without him? Bradford thought now. Squanto tells the Indians what we have to say and repeats their answers to us. He advises us in the way of the wilderness. Without Squanto we would not even know how to plant this corn.

He frowned. It troubled him to be planting seed that had been taken without payment. Massasoit had said that it must belong to the Nauset Indians who lived near Cornhill. Someday, Bradford thought, we must find those Indians and give them gifts for their corn.

He heard the sudden cry of a man in pain and turned to see Governor Carver staggering among the hills of soft earth. Bradford ran and helped the governor to a house where Elder Brewster and his wife sponged the sick man's head. It was all they knew to do for sunstroke.

A few days later John Carver died. The Pilgrims buried him in the best manner they could, with a few volleys of shot fired over his grave on the hill. Then the men gathered to elect a new governor, for they needed a leader without delay.

Elder William Brewster, who had been their leader in England and Holland, could not be chosen, for he was the teacher and leader of the church in the absence of Pastor Robinson. The Pilgrims had seen too much trouble in England from a mixture of church and state. They wanted true separation, a good governor who was not an officer of the church.

Unanimously they chose William Bradford, who had grown up in Brewster's home and who assumed more and more of the work and responsibility of the colony every day. They elected Allerton as Governor Bradford's assistant, and they stated a few simple rules of government.

The governor would carry out the day-to-day business and plans, and he had the authority to call upon any man for a particular assignment. But all the men would meet together to discuss and vote upon any really important decision affecting the welfare of the whole town. Government by consent of the governed in *town meetings*.

"God give me strength and wisdom to do what is best for the colony," Governor Bradford prayed that evening when he was alone. For it was one thing to know and do what he believed to be right for himself. It was quite another problem to have the vision to direct the welfare of all these people.

He began to think about the men he could trust and depend upon. There was Elder Brewster, of course, whom he had always loved and respected and could turn to for advice. Edward Winslow was only twenty-six but he had proved to be the best diplomat among them. The very day his young wife died, Edward had placed the safety of the colony above his own grief and gone to Massasoit's village as a hostage. He was patient, persuasive, and intelligent, always finding the right words and ideas to bring about friendly relations with others.

Captain Miles Standish, who had lost his wife too, was a courageous man who kept the men trained to defend the colony.

Samuel Fuller, while not a doctor, knew more about treating illnesses with herbs and kindly nursing than anyone else.

Bradford had always liked young John Alden, who had decided to stay with the Pilgrims, perhaps because he was interested in Priscilla Mullins, whose entire family had died that winter.

Stephen Hopkins was another man he could count on. The Hopkins family was one of the few fortunate families whose members had all lived through the winter. It seemed good to see a man, his wife, and four children alive and well.

There were two more whole families, the Brewsters and the Billingtons. William Bradford could understand why the Lord had spared the Brewsters, but the Billingtons were a most troublesome family from the slums of London, who had been allowed on the *Mayflower* by Thomas Weston's Adventurers. He shook his head over the Billingtons.

Then, when the corn had grown knee-high, seven-year-old John Billington did something worthwhile for the colony.

John and his nine-year-old brother, Francis, had been in trouble from the day they set foot on the ship. They had almost blown up the *Mayflower*, while she was anchored in the harbor off Cape Cod, by shooting off muskets near an open keg of powder.

All the children of Plymouth had been warned not to wander into the woods alone, for the Pilgrims knew very little as yet about the wilderness around them. In spite of the warning, John went exploring and could not find his way home. He walked for five days, living on berries and sleeping on the ground. Finally he came upon some Indians who could understand nothing he said, and, of course, he could not understand them. They took him to their canoe and rowed far away over the water.

When the boy did not return to Plymouth, Governor Bradford was concerned as well as angry, and sent Squanto to Massasoit to ask if the Indians had seen John Billington. Massasoit sent runners to many tribes. After some weeks, the chief reported that John was living with a tribe of Nausets on Cape Cod, the very Indians whose corn had been taken by the Pilgrims.

Governor Bradford sent men in the shallop to get John and to invite the Nauset Indians to come to Plymouth and make peace with the Pilgrim colony as Massasoit had done. The Indians of Cape Cod, who had always run away when they saw white men before, now came with the shallop bringing John home.

The governor looked at the boy in exasperation mixed with thankfulness. God works in mysterious ways, he thought.

The Nauset Indians ate with the Pilgrims and made a treaty of peace. Bradford gave them gifts to their satisfaction for the corn taken at Cornhill.

That night Governor Bradford heard the wind rustle the tassels and leaves of the twenty acres of corn growing at Plymouth and he slept better knowing the Indians had been paid for the seed.

6

Young Father
of the Colony

As governor, William Bradford's days were filled with problems to solve, great and small. He appointed men to hunt and others to fish to supplement the small ration of food from the storehouse. For no matter who did the work, all food and supplies were shared alike by the members of the colony. This was the agreement Thomas Weston and the other Adventurers had forced the Pilgrims to sign before they left Holland. All Pilgrims must work for a common fund, and no one could own private property for seven years, or until the Adventurers had been repaid all the money, including interest, that they had invested to help the Pilgrims reach America.

The new governor felt keenly the responsibility of paying the debt to the Adventurers and, at the same time, keeping the colony well and safe. God expects every man to live with a purpose to his life, he thought. It is my task, with the Lord's direction, to do what is best for Plymouth.

Whenever men could be spared from working in the fields or from hunting or fishing, Governor Bradford sent them to the woods to cut clapboards, or plank lumber, to be stored and sent back to England.

He attended to the trade with Massasoit. From the day the Wampanoag Indians made a peace treaty with the Pilgrims, they came frequently to Plymouth and brought beaver and otter skins to trade for small mirrors, beads, and knives. Often the Indians stayed in the village hoping to be invited to eat with their new friends.

At last Bradford sent Edward Winslow and Stephen Hopkins, with Squanto as their interpreter, to Massasoit. They told the chief that he and his Indians were welcome to come any time to trade at Plymouth, but the Pilgrims regretted that they had so little food they could not offer any to the Indians.

Gravely Massasoit nodded that he understood. "This is a great embarrassment which I often suffer," he said. "Even now my people have nothing to eat. I have sent men to fish, but for days few bass have come into these waters.

"As for my men," the chief added, "they will come when they have beaver but will no longer pester you. And that we may have better understanding, I do appoint Hobomok, a member of my war council and one of the chief men among us, to go and live at Plymouth. Hobomok shall go back and forth between us to increase goodwill for both of us."

Bradford found Hobomok to be a strong, courageous young Indian with good judgment. He attached himself to Captain Standish, as Squanto had to Bradford.

Soon the governor had a duty he enjoyed. He performed the marriage of his friend Edward Winslow to Mrs. Susan White, whose husband had died in the winter's sickness and left her with two small boys. Now there were four families Bradford could ask to adopt the youngest orphaned children of the colony. The older girls of the village were already taking turns helping to look after the motherless children.

During the summer the carpenter, Francis Eaton, and John Alden, with the help of the older boys, built seven plank houses with thatched roofs as well as storehouses and the common house. At last Bradford was able to assign a place for each Pilgrim to live although the few small houses were crowded.

The governor was also judge for the colony and one of his first decisions was to hand down the punishment for a duel fought by Edward Leister and Edward Dotey, bond servants of

Stephen Hopkins. Both young men had fallen in love with pretty fifteen-year-old Constance Hopkins.

The sound of their shouts and the noise of sword against dagger brought Miles Standish on a run to the beach where the quarrel was taking place. When he brought the two men before Governor Bradford, the captain's anger made his face almost as red as his hair.

Bradford lectured them. "The colony needs every pair of hands if it is to survive," he said. "No one has a right to endanger his life, for in so doing he endangers the life of every one of us."

He ordered the two Edwards to be bound with their heads and heels tied together until their anger cooled. Soon they were so uncomfortable that they cried for mercy, and he let them go.

Sometimes it seemed to William Bradford that he had grown older than his thirty-one years. He felt like the father of a large family that he must feed and protect and discipline.

Bradford's assistant, Isaac Allerton, although four years older than the governor, did not want to bother with the domestic problems of the colony. He liked trade and business.

In mid-September, Bradford sent Allerton, with Stephen Hopkins and other men, in the shallop to Massachusetts Bay to trade with the Massachusetts Indians there. The men returned with good furs which were stored along with the furs bought from Massasoit's Indians. Bradford looked at the full storehouse in gratitude, for he planned to send the many fine beaver and otter skins to England on the next visiting ship as part payment to the Adventurers.

In October the corn was ready to harvest. Governor Bradford walked in the fields and fingered the heavy ears in their drying husks. If the Pilgrims were careful, there was enough corn to last through the coming winter.

He looked across the field at the row of small houses which sheltered them now. How cold they had been last winter and how sick. A summer of sun had helped them recover their health and strength. The men were catching many fat cod, bass, and other fish. Wild ducks and geese had begun their flight from the north and often settled down in the ponds and brook. There were wild turkeys in the woods too, so the hunting had improved, although it was still difficult to hit game with their old muskets.

All summer there has been no want, thanks be to God, he thought. He hoped the coming winter would be much better than the last.

He glanced at the woods bordering the field. How beautiful were the oaks and maples turning red and gold against the evergreens. In Leyden at this time of year, the Dutch had always held a feast of thanksgiving for their deliverance from the Spaniards. He remembered, too, the harvest feasts in the villages of England.

He would declare a feast to thank God for the Pilgrims' deliverance from sickness and hunger. A Thanksgiving feast. For the first time they had enough food to invite guests. They would invite Massasoit and some of his men to the celebration.

Joyfully the Pilgrims harvested the corn together, peeled back the husks and tied the corn in bunches to the rafters of the common house to dry. They squeezed the juice from wild grapes, which Bradford tasted and pronounced very sweet and strong. The children gathered wild plums and watercress and wild leeks for salads.

When the day of Thanksgiving arrived, the women turned roasts on spits in fireplaces and over outdoor fires. Men set up plank tables under the trees. The children helped carry food to the tables and got in everyone's way and tripped over the one little dog in the colony, who barked to add to the excitement.

Massasoit came with ninety braves and also brought five deer shot with bow and arrow. Captain Miles Standish marched his men with drum and trumpet to entertain the Indians and to impress them, too, with the Pilgrims' strength. The Indians danced as they did at harvesttime in their villages. The Pilgrim and Indian men played games of skill and strength, enjoyed races and shooting. The feasting continued for three days.

When the Indians returned home, Governor Bradford counted

the supply of food remaining in the common house. He had not expected Massasoit to bring such a large company of men. But the Thanksgiving feast had been a happy time for all, Pilgrims and Indians alike, and their friendship and trust had increased. If he portioned the corn carefully, there would be about a peck of cornmeal for each person to last until the next year's harvest.

A few weeks later Governor Bradford was seated at the large plank table that he used as a desk when it was not in use for dining. He was writing in his journal, for he was keeping a record of the life at Plymouth. He did not want men to forget the Pilgrims' hope for freedom in beginning here, even if the little colony should perish. Edward Winslow, too, often wrote letters to describe the countryside and the plans of the colony. Their letters would be sent to friends in England and Holland on the first ship that might visit here.

The governor was startled by an Indian who came running into his house. Squanto, who was never very far from Bradford, followed the strange Indian and interpreted his words. A ship, a white man's ship, had been seen off Cape Cod. It was sailing toward Plymouth.

Bradford called together the men with whom he often discussed larger problems: Brewster, Standish, Allerton, Fuller, Winslow, and Hopkins. "We are not expecting a ship," he said. "It could be from the French settlement in Canada sent to try to capture the colony, or it could be pirates. We must not lose our food or furs."

The men agreed, and Governor Bradford ordered the cannon on the hill to be fired to bring in all the men from work in the woods or from fishing. Captain Standish called them to arms for defense in case it was necessary. But when the ship finally came into Plymouth harbor, the watching Pilgrims saw that its flag was the red cross of England, an unexpected ship from home.

Bradford rejoiced with all the other Pilgrims when a longboat pulled ashore and they saw Robert Cushman among the men in it. He was one of the Pilgrims who had made the arrangements with the Adventurers in London for the *Mayflower*

voyage. Quickly the governor called his small council together
to hear the news from home.

Deacon Cushman sat on the governor's right at the plank
table where the council was seated. "Our ship, the *Fortune*,
brought thirty-five persons to add to the colony," he said.
"Thomas Weston's Adventurers recruited the men whose ways
are not our ways, but they are young and strong.

"Weston has asked me to return with the *Fortune* at once and
bring the furs and corn and any other payment you have ready
for our London investors."

"We have many fine furs," Bradford said. "And we have cut
good clapboard in every moment we could spare, for we know
lumber is worth a good price in England. But we cannot spare
corn. We have scarcely enough to last us through the winter."

"The Adventurers will welcome the payment of furs and
lumber," Cushman said, "although they will be disappointed
at the size of your corn harvest. At least you will have enough
to supply the ship on its journey home. We brought little food
expecting to find corn here for our return."

Governor Bradford looked at his council and saw that they
were as astonished as he was at Cushman's request. An even
more terrible suspicion came to him.

"What have these newcomers brought with them to eat during the winter?" he asked.

"They have come to live at Plymouth Plantation," Cushman
answered. "They expect to share your food as well as your
work."

"Have they brought bedding?" Bradford asked. "And pots
and pans to cook their meat in? Have they coats and clothes
enough to wear against the cold? We have no clothing in Plymouth except what we brought on the *Mayflower* and much of
that is worn and patched now."

"They will work," Deacon Cushman said again.

The governor saw that Cushman, although one of their own
people, could not really understand how alone the Pilgrims
were here, how desperate their situation would be if their sup-

plies ran out. There was nothing he could do except be thankful for the additional strength of thirty-five persons to the colony.

"We wish them better furnished with provisions," he said at last, "but that cannot be helped now."

In a few days Governor Bradford stood beside Edward Winslow as the Pilgrims watched the *Fortune* set out for England. The ship carried letters from both men. Bradford had written urging Weston and the other Adventurers to send supplies to Plymouth. He had sent letters to friends in Holland, among them one to Pastor Robinson asking about his little son. He hoped someday to send for John when he had a home for him.

The sails of the *Fortune* billowed in the breeze, and Winslow said, "She's heavy laden. What do you think the cargo we loaded on her is worth?"

"It was good clapboard," Bradford answered, "and two hogsheads of beaver and otter skins of a very fine grade. I reckon the entire worth at five hundred pounds, enough to pay half our entire debt to the Adventurers."

Edward Winslow was as pleased as his friend. "Another shipload like that and our debt will be paid."

Bradford smiled. "Then we will be free to own land for ourselves."

7

Hunger

After the departure of the *Fortune*, Governor Bradford and his assistant, Allerton, made an exact count of the food in the storehouse.

"I wrote to Thomas Weston," Bradford said, "and told him how little food we have and urged him to send provisions as soon as possible."

"Still, we cannot expect a ship with supplies before spring," Allerton said, "and there is scarcely enough food to keep our own people alive through the winter, to say nothing of Weston's newcomers."

"Then," Bradford said, "I must order rations of half-allowance to everyone, old comers and new alike."

Bradford had scarcely assigned room in the crowded houses to the thirty-five uninvited additions to the colony when a strange Indian brave ran down the street of Plymouth. He carried a bundle of arrows tied with a snakeskin and he called for the governor. Bradford appeared, and the Indian flung the arrows to the ground at the governor's feet.

Bradford called a council and sent for Squanto and Hobomok to interpret the Indian messenger's words.

"He is a brave from the Narraganset tribe," Squanto explained to the small group of men seated at the plank table. "His tribe lives on the western shore of Narragansett Bay and has as many braves as the sands of the sea."

Bradford was used to Squanto's desire to be important which sometimes led to exaggeration. Still, the Narragansets were a very strong tribe that had never shown unfriendliness before. He looked at Hobomok.

"Arrows tied with a snakeskin are a threat of war," Hobomok said.

"The Narragansets know that many new strong men came on a ship," Squanto added. "Their chief asks, how many men come? How much land they take now?"

The governor turned to his council. Miles Standish spoke quickly. "If we show fear, the Indians will attack us, and there are hundreds of them to one of us."

The men agreed. Bradford picked up the snakeskin and stuffed it with musketballs and sent it back to the chief of the Narragansets with a message.

"If the Narragansets would rather have war than peace," he said, "then they may begin when they will. The Pilgrims have done them no harm, neither do we fear them. If the Narragansets come, they will find this colony ready."

The messenger took the snakeskin stuffed with bullets to the Narragansets. Their chief would not touch it, but returned it again to Plymouth.

This meant there would be no fighting, yet Governor Bradford decided it was wise to build a stockade around the houses, to lock the gates at night and post guards. Every able-bodied man in the colony was set to work to build an eleven-foot-high fence of long poles driven into the ground. The poles were woven together at the top with tough wild vines gathered from the woods by the women and children.

The work would take all winter, for the stockade was to run up from the beach along the north bank of Town Brook, include the hill where the Pilgrims planned to build a fort, then back down to the beach. It enclosed enough of the clearing so that every house had a garden spot within the walls where the families could grow vegetables, herbs, and flowers.

On Christmas Day, Governor Bradford went as usual to work

on the stockade and found only the Pilgrim men working. He went to the houses to call out the young men who had come on the *Fortune*. The newcomers said they were Church of England men. It was against their conscience to work on Christmas Day.

Bradford remembered that, one year ago, Christmas had been the first day of work in Plymouth, when the Pilgrim men had laid the foundation for their common house. That night when the men returned to the *Mayflower*, Captain Jones had offered them Christmas cheer in the old English manner. The Pilgrims did not believe in celebrating Christmas but they had been grateful for Captain Jones's food and cheer after their hard day of work.

"If it is a matter of your conscience," Bradford said at last to the newcomers, "then we will spare you today."

At noon Bradford and the other Pilgrim men walked home for lunch. They came upon the newcomers playing games in the street. Some pitched a bar to see who could throw farthest. Others played stoolball.

Bradford stood a moment listening to the young men's shouts and laughter. He looked at the tired faces of the men beside him, at the blisters on Elder Brewster's hands. Brewster was the oldest man in the colony, yet he labored every day except the Sabbath, when he taught God's Word to the Pilgrims gathered at his home.

Governor Bradford went to the newcomers and took their bar and the ball. "If Christmas is a matter of devotion to you," he said, "then keep to your houses. There will be no more reveling in the streets, for it is against *my* conscience that you should play while others work."

The stockade was completed by spring. It was a good thing, Bradford thought, for by this time famine was a real threat, and the people were so weak they could scarcely work. Eagerly they watched the sea for sight of a sail, hoping that the Adventurers had sent food.

"The *Fortune* carried such a large shipment in payment of our debts," Bradford assured the people, "that Thomas Weston should be generous with the supplies he promised to furnish us."

The governor was eager to accumulate another large store of furs to be sent in payment on the next boat, but he ran into difficulty with Massasoit. The chief was angry with Squanto and would no longer allow his Indians to come back and forth to Plymouth to trade.

When Bradford ignored the requests of Indian messengers for Squanto to be turned over to them, Massasoit himself appeared at Plymouth Plantation and demanded that Squanto be given to him to be put to death. The governor invited the great chief to sit and eat what little food he could offer.

"Squanto is not here," Bradford explained through Hobomok. "I sent him on the shallop with ten of my men to trade furs with the Indians at Massachusetts Bay. Tell me what Squanto has done to offend you."

"Squanto brags that he is greater than Massasoit," the chief said. "He has made my braves fear him, so that they listen to Squanto instead of to me. They even give *him* gifts to keep peace with *you*."

"We are your friends," the governor said. "You have nothing to fear from us."

"Squanto tells my braves that you have the plague which killed all his tribe. He says you have the plague buried in your storehouse, and Squanto can send it amongst us if he wishes, for he claims to have much influence upon you."

"We have no plague anywhere, and Squanto could not turn us against you," Bradford assured the chief. "He only wanted to seem important to your braves."

Massasoit was too enraged to be pacified. He went home. But when the Pilgrims' shallop returned from Massachusetts Bay, the chief sent another messenger to bring Squanto to the Indian village.

Again Bradford pleaded for Squanto's life. "He deserves some kind of punishment, for he lied and undermined the authority of the chief," Bradford agreed. "But for our sakes, spare

Squanto. Hobomok is not always with us. How can we understand Massasoit or any of the Indians without Squanto?"

The messenger returned with this answer but Massasoit sent several leading braves to Plymouth. They tossed fine beaver skins on the plank table before Bradford. Hobomok interpreted their words.

"Massasoit sent beaver skins. Now you will give us Squanto. The great chief sent his own knife, as our custom is. We will cut off Squanto's head and hands and bring them to Massasoit."

Governor Bradford thought fast. He had heard that the Narraganset Indians knew of Massasoit's anger. They hoped to take advantage of it and talk Massasoit into joining them in an attack on Plymouth. Could he risk the life of the entire colony to save Squanto? Perhaps he could think of some way to pacify the chief if he could gain some time.

"Take back the furs to Massasoit," Bradford said. "It is not the manner of the English to sell men's lives at a price."

The governor saw how angry the Indians were at his refusal and he lifted his hand to ask them to wait. Fond as he was of Squanto, he dared not anger Massasoit to war upon the colony. In this terrible choice, his own people must come first. He sent Hobomok to get Squanto, hoping his Indian friend would run away into the forest when he knew the danger. But Squanto came and stood before Bradford and the Indians who demanded his life.

He pleaded innocent. "Hobomok told the chief lies about me," Squanto said. "He is jealous that I am in favor with the governor."

"No, no," Hobomok denied. "Squanto bragged to all of his great power. He brought his own trouble upon him."

Bradford believed him. There was rivalry between the two Indians for the affection of the Pilgrims, yet both were trusted friends.

Squanto must have seen Bradford's problem, for he said, "I will not cause my governor trouble. I yield myself to be sent or not, according to what he thinks is best."

Silently Governor Bradford prayed for direction. In that instant men came running and said there was a ship passing the headland not far away. Bradford seized upon the coming ship as his excuse.

"I must go at once," he said to Massasoit's men, "to see if the ship brings enemies or friends. Later we will consider delivering Squanto to you."

The braves were insulted at the delay and went home in great anger.

The ship was small, only a shallop carrying seven men. It had sailed from a larger ship which Thomas Weston had sent to fish near the islands of Maine. The men brought no food but they gave Governor Bradford a letter from Weston.

Bradford read the letter aloud to Brewster, Winslow, Standish, and Allerton who had gone with him to Brewster's house. He paused and looked at his friends. "Not one word about the furs and clapboard sent on the *Fortune*," he said, "although Weston's letter is dated January 12, months after the *Fortune* would have reached England."

"The Adventurers have ignored the payment of half our debt," Brewster said, "as if we had sent nothing at all."

"Or the *Fortune* never reached England," Winslow suggested.

This was such a chilling thought that no one answered him. Bradford read another paragraph from Thomas Weston's letter:

We have sent this ship on our own account, and desire you will supply our men with such necessities as you can spare and they want. Among other things, we pray you to lend or sell them some seed corn. And if you have salt remaining from last year, that you let them have it for their present use.

"This is cold comfort to fill our hungry bellies," Miles Standish cried, his face flaming.

Governor Bradford too was angry that Weston had sent no supplies but only increased their burden by sending seven men to feed. These men were not even to work for the colony but intended to set up a post nearby and trade with the Indians for their own and Weston's profit.

"We need every kernel of corn to plant," the governor said, "then it will be months before it can be harvested, yet we cannot let men die."

Elder Brewster prayed for wisdom to know what to do to save so many persons from starvation. Surely, Bradford thought, the Lord, who has never failed us, will help us now.

A few weeks later Governor Bradford felt that the prayers had been answered when another small shallop came to Plymouth bringing a letter from the captain of a ship which was then fishing in waters off the coast of Maine. Captain John Huddleston did not know any of the Pilgrims, but his ship was from Virginia and he sent good wishes to them as neighbors. The captain wrote to warn Plymouth that the Indians had fallen upon the Virginia colony and massacred most of the settlers along the James River. Let the Pilgrims beware of their own safety.

Quickly the governor sent Edward Winslow with a few men on the Pilgrims' shallop to the Maine waters to visit the captain's ship. Winslow took furs to buy whatever food the Virginia ship could spare.

Captain Huddleston gave the Pilgrims hard bread or biscuit and would not take payment for it, saying he wished he had more to give. Winslow also brought back salted fish given by isolated settlers on the islands of Maine.

Bradford stored the biscuit and gave it out, a quarter of a pound daily to each person. He knew the people were so hungry that they might eat all the food at once, then starve before the harvest. With the biscuit and eels, which they tramped out in the mud along the creek, the Pilgrims lived and planted their precious seed corn a second spring. And they reelected William Bradford governor for another year.

About the first of July, when the corn had tasseled and young ears had begun to swell, two ships came into Plymouth harbor from England, the *Charity* and the *Swan.* They brought almost sixty men sent over by Thomas Weston to increase the fur trading post which he had had set up at Wessagusset on Massachusetts Bay in competition with the Pilgrims' trade with the Indians. These men, too, had no provisions but expected Plymouth to feed them.

Although the Pilgrims shared their food again with Weston's men, the newcomers slipped into the fields at night and stole the young sweet corn to eat. Bradford set a guard to save the corn for harvest.

With the Pilgrims in such distress, the governor decided it was not wise to tell them of another letter Weston had sent on the *Charity*. But he called his small council together and read them the bad news.

Weston wrote that the *Fortune* had finally arrived in England, but the ship had been robbed at sea by French pirates who had taken all her cargo. Naturally the Adventurers could not credit the Pilgrims with any payment, since their furs and clapboard had gone to the pirates.

"The *Fortune* was Weston's ship," Allerton said, "and his crew accepted our cargo, yet *we,* not *they,* owned the cargo when the pirates stole it!"

"The end of his letter brings an even greater shock," Bradford said. "The Adventurers have decided to break up the stock company. Although they agreed in Holland to send us supplies on credit as long as we needed them, they have sent none and will never send any now. But they expect the return of all the money they have loaned us."

Governor Bradford looked at the letter he held in his hand and read aloud: " 'I fear you must stand on your own legs, and trust, as they say, to God and yourselves. Your loving friend, Tho. Weston.' "

For a long moment the council was speechless, then Brewster said, "After all our hard work we owe as much as before. Even more, for the interest is high on our loan from the Adventurers."

"The loss of our cargo on the *Fortune* leaves us poor credit in England," Winslow said. "How shall we buy supplies?"

"Again our harvest will be too small to feed ourselves and all our uninvited guests," Standish said.

"Another winter of hunger will leave few of us alive," Brewster agreed. "With God's help, we will find a way."

"We must send another cargo soon," Bradford said. "Already we have some fine furs in storage."

"Weston's company is taking much of the fur trade from us," Allerton warned. "And we have run out of all manner of goods. We have nothing to give the Indians for their furs and corn."

Again it seemed to Bradford that God directed the next ship which came into Plymouth harbor. The *Discovery,* bound for England, stopped for a short visit after an unsuccessful trip to trade for furs in Virginia. The captain of the *Discovery* had a great store of beads and knives and other things for trade with the Indians. He was delighted when Bradford opened the Pilgrims' store of furs.

"But," the captain said, "I must charge very high prices for my stuff to make up for the disappointment of this trip."

The Pilgrims needed the trading goods so much that Bradford gave many fine beaver skins for them. He planned to take the new trading goods and go to Cape Cod, as soon as the harvest was in, to trade with the Nauset Indians there for all the corn they could spare from their fall crop.

Later when Weston's company of traders heard that Bradford was going to Cape Cod, they asked to go with him. They said they would sail their ship, the *Swan,* and share half-and-half whatever corn was bought.

The Pilgrims had no ship the size of the *Swan,* so Bradford agreed to the joint trip. He took Squanto with him as guide and interpreter. The master of the *Swan* was not familiar with the flats and breakers off Cape Cod and ran into trouble on the same shoals that had caused the *Mayflower* to turn back two years before.

The *Swan* put into Manamoyack Bay (Monomoy on the ocean side of Chatham) and many of the men went ashore in the ship's boat. At first the Indians of this place hid, for they were not of the tribes who knew the Pilgrims.

"We will camp here overnight," Bradford said. He sent Squanto to persuade the Indians that the strangers meant no harm but wanted to trade with them.

In the morning the Indians came to the camp. Bradford

bought eight hogsheads of corn and dried beans from them. While the supplies were being carried by small boat and loaded on the *Swan,* the governor saw Squanto lie down upon a mat on the ground as if he were sick. He went to him and found Squanto burning with fever.

Bradford brought water and sponged his friend's face and fed him a little broth, and prayed for him. Soon the master of the *Swan* came ashore and urged the governor to hurry and come aboard ship, for these were treacherous waters and he wanted to leave as soon as possible.

"Squanto is too sick to be moved," Bradford said. "We must wait until he is better."

Squanto grew weaker every day. Finally he knew that he could not live. He asked Bradford to give his knife and bow and arrows, his chieftain's headdress and white bone necklace, to his Pilgrim friends.

"And pray that I will enter your English heaven," Squanto said to Bradford, "for I always want to be with you."

The governor buried Squanto in the dunes of Cape Cod, in the manner in which he had buried so many of his Plymouth friends, with a prayer first and then a volley of shot fired over his grave.

Governor Bradford said, then, that the *Swan* must continue the search for corn in spite of the great loss of Squanto. He knew very little of the Indian languages but somehow he must make himself understood. The *Swan* rounded the tip of Cape Cod and sailed down the bay to Nauset where Bradford bought more corn and beans, and the Indians entertained him well.

The *Swan* sailed on to another Indian village (now Yarmouth) and lay offshore while Bradford and some of his men went to trade. A great and violent storm almost destroyed the *Swan* and cast the ship's small boat up on the beach so that both needed repairs to be safe.

Bradford sent word to the master of the *Swan* to return to Plymouth for repairs. He would continue his journey by land. He asked the Indians to stack the corn he had bought from them

and bring mats and cut sedge to cover the stacks. He told them
he would send the Pilgrims' shallop later to carry the corn home.

Then Bradford, with a few of his men and an Indian guide,
walked the fifty miles to Plymouth, stopping off at several Indian
villages along the way where he was treated kindly. He traded
for corn and beans and squash which he hoped would keep the
Pilgrims from starving until another harvest.

By March all the food bought on Cape Cod had been eaten.
Again the people elected William Bradford as governor of
Plymouth. He looked at the ninety gaunt men, women, and
children remaining alive after that third winter. Something had
to be done to plant more corn than before or the Pilgrims would
spend every winter in misery. He called his council together
around the rough plank table.

"I wish that all men were like you," the governor said to
Brewster, Standish, Winslow, and Hopkins, "but we have seen
that some men will not work if they know they can eat by the
labor of others."

The men at the table nodded. They had been forced by the
Adventurers to sign an agreement not to own or use property as
individuals until the Pilgrims had paid their debt to the stock-
holders.

"No matter how hard a man and his family work," Stephen
Hopkins said, "he owns nothing. He sees the work of his wife
and children go to feed those who fish and trap at their leisure."

"Men vary in abilities," Elder Brewster said gently. "Men of
lesser talents should eat, but men of greater talents should not
be discouraged by treating all alike."

"The Adventurers broke their promise to send us supplies,"
Edward Winslow said. "We owe them money but no obedience
now."

"We agree that planting for the common good has not been
satisfactory," Governor Bradford said. "I will accept the responsibility for breaking the agreement. From now on, every man
will raise his own corn. In all other things we will share in the
general way as before."

The council worked late by candlelight to assign each family a parcel of about one acre of land to plant, although the land itself continued to belong to the colony. The single men were placed with the small families to make an equal distribution.

As the Pilgrims planted corn the third spring, Bradford was pleased with the success of his plan. Everyone was industrious when he knew that the corn he raised would belong to him to use as he would. Even women, who before had pretended to be too weak, went to the fields and took their children to help them plant and hoe.

In late April, Bradford sat one night at the plank table. He felt too weak and tired to write much in his journal, yet he set down a few notes.

I have seen men stagger by reason of faintness for want of food. Such is our state as in the morning we often had our food to seek for the day, yet we performed the duties of our callings, I mean the other daily labors to provide for after-time.

He paused. Plymouth colony must not fail from starvation. The Pilgrims still wanted to remain in a free world with freedom of government and religion. How could they live through the months until harvest?

The Pilgrims had only one small boat. They were not seamen or even good fishermen. Yet, Bradford decided, he would divide the men into companies or gangs of six or seven men each. A gang would take the net and put to sea, and not come home until the boat had a load of bass or other fish. Then, at once, the next gang would set out.

All that season the desperate Pilgrims rivaled one another to see which gang could bring in the best catch. Even so, the boat often stayed out many days or returned with such a small catch that the Pilgrims on shore lived by digging shellfish at low tide from the sands. In this way they worked and endured until their third harvest.

8

Bradford's Family

On an early July evening William Bradford sat late on the stoop of his house, which was so newly built that he could smell the sap in its pine and spruce planks. The men had built the governor's house a little larger than the other eleven houses that made up Plymouth's main street. They said the governor must have room for his books and records and the plank trestle table around which the council met. On the hill above, they had built a square log fort as a place for worship and for town meetings as well as for defense.

William Bradford was proud of the town the Pilgrims were building but he wondered what Alice Southworth would think of it, if she did come here to marry him. He remembered Alice so well. She was his age and had grown up near him in England, then had moved to Leyden with early Separatists. There she had married Edward Southworth, a wealthy silk-weaver, shortly before William Bradford had married Dorothy May.

A year ago friends on the ship *Charity* had told Bradford that Edward Southworth was dead. The governor had written Alice a letter and asked her to come to Plymouth to marry him. Alice had a sister in Plymouth, Deacon Fuller's wife. Another sister was coming with her husband, George Morton, and family on the ship *Anne*, which the Pilgrims had been expecting for days. He hoped Alice would come, yet he was suddenly fearful that she might not like what she saw.

He heard footsteps and Elder Brewster came around the corner of the house and sat on the stoop beside him. "I saw that you had not blown out your rushlight," the older man said. "I cannot sleep either, for thinking of the *Anne* so long past due and the fate of my daughters and our friends on board."

"How can I think," Bradford said, "that Alice will want to exchange her fine home for this? What little furniture we have is rough with marks of the adze. While she—"

"Alice knew you as a boy searching for what you believed to be right," Elder Brewster said gently. "She saw you begin to grow in responsibility in Holland. She will be proud of what you have done for this colony, for we are the only group of people who have been able to survive in the new world without being supplied by a mother country."

"We have built the colony together," William Bradford said. "Even the children have worked hard."

"We have all worked with devotion," the older man agreed, "but we could have given up many times without your unbending purpose. You made us realize we must depend upon ourselves if we are to survive.

"You are governor, Will. You have been chosen each spring by vote of the people. Any woman would be proud of that trust in you."

He paused. Bradford could tell by the tone of Elder Brewster's voice that he smiled. "And Alice may love you, Will, even as we do."

William Bradford felt deeply moved by affection for the older man. "I am wrong to despair," he said, "when the Lord has been so good to us. I will get out my best suit with the silver buckles, and my violet velvet cape. If your good wife will be so kind as to mend them, I'll be ready if Alice comes."

Fourteen days later the *Anne* sailed into Plymouth harbor. All the Pilgrims left their work and ran to the beach to wave and call to those coming ashore in the longboat. Elder Brewster and his wife wept to see their daughters, Patience and Fear. "They have grown up in these four years," Mrs. Brewster cried.

Then William Bradford saw Alice Southworth among the passengers and silently thanked God. With her were her sister and husband and their five children, the youngest a baby a few weeks old. She had left her own two young sons in Holland. William welcomed them all and invited the George Morton family to move into his house until they could build a home of their own. He had scarcely shown them and Alice to his door, when he left to find places to live for the sixty new members of the colony. Many of the passengers on the *Anne* were wives and children of the Pilgrims or old friends, and they had brought clothing and food which would help feed everyone until the harvest.

A month later, August 14, 1623, William Bradford married Alice Southworth. Even the children of Plymouth came to the brief civil ceremony at the Fort, which was followed by refreshments served under the trees. There was laughter and happy visiting among the Pilgrims and their friends.

The guests admired Alice's gown with the purple skirt looped in front to show her lacy petticoat, and the beautiful things she brought to the governor's house with her. They fingered the elegant damask tablecloths, the fine Holland pillowbeers and towels. Trenchers of pewter and of wood, even damask napkins and silver spoons! A great silver loving cup, a grand cup holding two quarts, which had been given to Bradford by Governor Carver's wife just before she died, was passed from friend to friend around the table, and each took a deep swallow to toast the bride and groom.

Even Massasoit and several of his men were among the guests, for the chief was the Pilgrims' friend again. Not long before, he had been so ill that he was expected to die. Bradford had sent Edward Winslow to the Indian village with herbs for medicine and with chickens to make broth for the chief. Winslow had tended the chief until he recovered, and Massasoit never forgot that the Pilgrims saved his life.

William Bradford had always thought of Plymouth colony as one large family. Now with its increased size he wanted to find

new sources of food and income for the people. He sent Edward
Winslow on the *Anne,* when she returned to England, with furs
to buy livestock for Plymouth. The next spring Winslow returned with the first cattle in the colony, three heifers and a bull.

Two years later, Governor Bradford heard that members of a
small settlement on Maine's Monhegan Island had decided to
break up and return to England. He and Winslow with a crew
sailed the shallop filled with furs to buy from the Monhegan
settlers. They bought goats and pigs for Plymouth.

When the livestock had increased in number, the Pilgrims
asked Bradford for the right to use more lands for grazing and
planting. The men said the harvests were good now, there was
plenty of seed corn. They wanted to branch out from the small
fields of Plymouth and settle farms and villages nearby.

Bradford was alarmed at the thought of losing any of the
colonists, yet he saw that the growing families needed the use
of more land. But under the terms of the agreement with the
Adventurers, he had no right to grant it.

About the same time, the Adventurers sent more letters of
protest saying that Plymouth colony was not paying off its debt
fast enough. Bradford compared his careful accounts with their
demands. He was shocked to find that the Adventurers charged
such a high price for the use of every ship they sent to get the
furs and clapboard that the Pilgrims' debt was almost as large
as it had been in the beginning. The governor sent his assistant,
Allerton, to England to ask the Adventurers to set a definite final
sum that the Pilgrims owed. For, he wrote, someway the Pilgrims must be set free from this strangling debt or Plymouth
could never prosper.

While William Bradford waited through the winter for Allerton's return with an answer from the Adventurers, he was busy
with his own family, which now filled the governor's house with
young people of many ages.

He and Alice had been happy at the birth of their son, another
William Bradford, a year after their marriage. Now they had a
new baby, their daughter Mercy, who was a joy to everyone.

The five Morton children still lived with them, for their father had died soon after arriving in Plymouth on the *Anne*. Nathaniel Morton, Alice's oldest nephew, was a great help to Bradford in keeping the records of the government.

Alice's two sons, Constant and Thomas Southworth, and Bradford's own son, John, had come from Leyden. Somehow Alice had found room for everyone including four older boys Bradford had taken care of since their parents died in the sickness of the first winter, Thomas Cushman, Joseph Rogers, William Latham, and Samuel Cuthbertson.

William Bradford took as much time as he could from his many duties to teach the boys to read and write. "I hope you may grow up loving to learn," he said, "but more important, I wish you to be aware of the real values in life; honesty, charity, with kindness and affection for one another."

9

A Pilgrim Saddle
on a Bay Horse

In the spring of 1627, Assistant Governor Allerton returned from England with an answer from the Adventurers. They offered the Pilgrims a "bargain." They would free the Pilgrims absolutely from all debts for the sum of 1800 pounds sterling, to be paid 200 pounds each year for nine years.

That night William Bradford sat late at the plank table reviewing his accounts. There were 180 persons in Plymouth including the children. They had thirty-two houses. The Pilgrims could not be sure of an income any year, for they had very little to depend upon—their corn, the wood they cut, and a small trade in furs with the Indians.

The next day he called together his small council. "To undertake to pay so much money in nine years is a great risk," the governor said, "but if we accept the Adventurers' 'bargain,' we shall be free of any outside control. We can apply for a land patent in our own name and can divide the land as the men are asking us to do."

"If the land is given outright to the people," Miles Standish asked, "how shall we pay the debt?"

"We will continue to own the fur trade in common until the debt is paid," the governor said.

"We would have to increase the fur trade greatly," Allerton said, "to raise 200 pounds sterling a year."

"We must find a way," Brewster said.

Governor Bradford called a meeting at the Fort to put the plan before the people. After much discussion, the men agreed that each voter in Plymouth would become a *Purchaser* of the colony's debt. Each man would purchase one share, and the share would also entitle him to about twenty acres of land. Men were named (a committee) to divide the land near the town into shares as equal as possible in value. The shares were then drawn by lot so that no man could say that others were favored by a better location of land than his.

Governor Bradford now considered the best way to increase the fur trade in order to pay off the debt that hung so heavily upon the Purchasers. He planned to establish trading posts near the Indians in Maine, Connecticut, Rhode Island, and on Cape Cod. Someone had to take out the patents for the trading posts. Someone had to accept the costs and responsibility for acquiring land and rights to posts in the various places. Someone had to supply trading goods, keep accounts, ship the furs to England for sale.

Again Governor Bradford called the men of the colony together. He told them clearly how much greater their debt must be to increase trade and pay the 200 pounds a year owed to the Adventurers. The Purchasers were alarmed at the new expenses, and the governor suggested a plan to them.

Bradford, Allerton, and Standish would undertake the new expenses and pay off the entire debt of the colony if (1) the voters granted the *Undertakers* the right to all the colony's trade, and (2) each land-shareholder paid the Undertakers three bushels of corn or six pounds of tobacco yearly.

After some discussion the Purchasers were eager to place the burden of debt on the shoulders of the few Undertakers. In this way each man knew exactly what he owed yearly, and his tax was small for such peace of mind.

Soon after, the three Undertakers took in other partners to help expand the fur trade: Winslow, Brewster, and three younger men, Thomas Prence, John Alden, and John Howland.

Governor Bradford was anxious to make sure that the Pilgrims held a legal right to the land they had explored and settled. Again he sent Allerton to England to apply for a patent. In 1629, after much effort and expense, a royal patent was granted in the name of Governor William Bradford by the Council for New England and signed by Sir Ferdinando Gorges and the Earl of Warwick. William Bradford was so busy that he scarcely thought of the fact that the patent made him legal owner of all Plymouth Plantation including Cape Cod.

Within a year, Bradford faced the first real political threat to Plymouth in the arrival of a large colony of neighbors to the north at Massachusetts Bay. While Bradford had been busy with the problems of his small colony, a prosperous group of English Puritans under Governor Endicott had made a settlement they named Salem. Now, two years later (1630), a thousand Puritans, headed by Governor John Winthrop, sailed into Massachusetts Bay and landed at Charlestown.

Like the Pilgrims ten years before, the Bay's Puritans were sick with the fever that comes after such a long journey by ship. When Bradford heard that many of the Puritans were dying and only a few were well enough to tend the others, he sent the Pilgrims' own man of medicine, Samuel Fuller, to help them. The Pilgrims had little medicine for Deacon Fuller to take, but he knew the use of Indian herbs and with these he treated the sick Puritans. He also helped them by his kindness and assurance. He stayed for weeks in Charlestown and told the Puritans of the free form of government the Pilgrims had founded and their congregational way in religion. As the sick Puritans began to recover, they asked him more and more about the Pilgrims' way of greater freedom in worship and in town meetings.

At last Samuel Fuller wrote to his brother-in-law, Bradford, and said he thought his mission was accomplished and he would soon come home. He added, "We have some enemies in the Bay, but (blessed be God) more friends. The Governor is a godly, wise, and humble gentleman, and very discreet, and of a fine and good temper."

Bradford considered Fuller's description of the Bay's Governor John Winthrop and tried to be less suspicious of the richer and much larger colony, although he knew Puritans had never been as tolerant of other people's religious beliefs as were the Pilgrims. Moreover the Bay was not far away and it, too, wanted land and trade with the Indians.

Not long afterward, Governor Bradford was alarmed further when a small ship from Salem was forced to take refuge in Plymouth harbor in a storm. The Puritan captain admitted that he had been on his way to Cape Cod to trade with the Indians for corn.

Swiftly Bradford wrote the governor of the Bay Colony saying that Cape Cod was Pilgrim territory. The Pilgrims were the first to explore it and make friends with the Indians there. Cape Cod was a part of Plymouth Plantation to which Governor Bradford held a patent.

"Plymouth will resist any interference on Cape Cod," Bradford wrote, "even to the spending of our lives."

Having sent such a sharp rebuke to the Bay Colony, Governor Bradford decided to visit Governor Winthrop and see for himself what these neighbors were like. In the fall, when Bradford's good friend Captain Pierce of the ship *Lion* arrived in Plymouth harbor, Bradford asked the captain to take him and some of the leading Pilgrim men to Charlestown.

Alice Bradford brushed her husband's doublet and fluffed the ruff and wrist ruffles which had been stored in a chest so long. "Be sure your hair is well set up when you meet Governor Winthrop," she said.

He laughed at her, but he was well aware that it was important for him to look his best, to wear his long magistrate's robe and do justice to the office of governor of the first New England colony.

The two young governors, nearly the same age, liked each other at once. It was easy perhaps for each to recognize wisdom, strength, and leadership in each other.

Governor Winthrop held a dinner to introduce Bradford to

the magistrates of the Bay Colony. Governor Endicott of Salem came and also Sir Richard Saltonstall, among others. They ate and talked far into the night. Bradford was eager to hear all the news from England and know the plans of the Bay Colony.

Governor Winthrop told him that the Bay was going to move from Charlestown to a new location. "Several years ago," Winthrop said, "an Englishman made a solitary settlement on a peninsula he calls Trimountain, across the mouth of the Mystic River from us. There he has a cabin and an apple orchard and a fine spring of water. He offered to share his peninsula with us since it is so much more healthful than our present location. I am having my own frame house, which is partially built, taken down and set up close to his spring of water. Our entire Bay Colony will move there, and we will call it Boston."

Bradford shared some of his own problems and concerns with the Bay governor and the other magistrates. "John Billington, who has always been troublesome," he said, "murdered John Newcomin for trapping on land which Billington considered his own trapping ground although he had no legal right to it. We gave Billington a trial by jury and convicted him of willful murder, for he did lie in wait for Newcomin and shot him deliberately. The jury convicted Billington with no plea of mercy. It is my duty to sentence him to hang.

"His is the first such offense in Plymouth," Bradford continued. "I confess I have put off too long declaring his sentence, for I cannot pronounce the words to take a man's life. We have no lawyers in Plymouth. You were trained for the law. What would you do?"

"You must show a stern example to save future lives," Governor Winthrop answered, "then men will know the cost of murder."

When Governor Bradford left the Bay, he invited Governor Winthrop to return his visit. It was two years before Winthrop's duties in settling Boston permitted him to visit Plymouth in the fall of 1632.

Excitement ran high among the Pilgrims when the tall, aristocratic governor of the powerful Bay Colony, with his attendants, marched down the street of Plymouth to Governor Bradford's house. Alice Bradford had everything ready. Logs burned briskly in the great fireplace. A feast was laid out on the long plank table in the parlor.

Governor Bradford was careful to seat Governors Winthrop and Endicott and their pastor, Wilson, the table's length away from the Pilgrims' new church-teacher, Roger Williams. Bradford liked young Williams and had accepted him at Plymouth after Winthrop banished him for refusing certain demands of the Puritan Church.

After the long dinner, Winthrop looked at Bradford's shelves of books and expressed astonishment that the governor of Plymouth was studying Hebrew and knew Latin and Greek. Governor Bradford had even begun to write a history of Plymouth Plantation. How could he find the time?

"I wish our children to know their beginning," Bradford told him.

On Sunday, Winthrop and his party attended services in the Meetinghouse-Fort, and were impressed by the way in which the men of the congregation spoke on religious questions.

"You speak your minds even more freely," Winthrop said, "than Deacon Fuller told us when he came to tend our sick."

After a week's visit when they had feasted and had been entertained kindly every day at several houses, Governor Winthrop and his party left Plymouth very early in the morning. Bradford, Brewster, and several other men walked a half mile with them toward their ship anchored up the coast.

Bradford and Brewster stood together on the beach and watched their visitors depart in the longboat. Finally Brewster said, "It went well, Will."

"Yes," Bradford said dryly. "Governor Endicott informed me that he found us much more pleasing and enlightened than he had heard us to be."

Brewster laughed. "Puritan tact," he said. Then the older man's face softened. "I have thanked the Lord many times, Will," he said, "that a farm boy from Austerfield came into Scrooby Tavern and we welcomed him."

There was no doubt, Governor Bradford thought as he heard Elder Brewster leave for home, that the exchange of visits had brought the two English colonies closer together. Then why did he have such an uneasy feeling? What had the Pilgrims to fear from the bigger, richer, stricter Bay Colony?

Bradford thought he was alone, until Roger Williams spoke. "You noticed that Governor Winthrop disapproved of my presence here?" the young teacher asked, as he walked beside Bradford.

"Aye," William Bradford said, "but Winthrop is not governor of Plymouth."

"Take care that he will not be someday," Roger Williams said. "Have you heard how the Bay Colony treated the settler who so generously offered the Puritans a home on his peninsula?"

Bradford shook his head.

"The Bay moved in and took it all," Williams said, "then magnanimously voted to return fifty acres to the settler. He finally moved away."

"We shall not move, no matter how far they crowd us," Bradford said. "We paid too high a price for this ground."

Roger Williams smiled as though he were enjoying a secret joke.

"Governor Winthrop may not realize it," he said, "but you have already won a great spiritual victory. You have placed a Pilgrim saddle on the Bay horse."

Bradford smiled too. It was true that the Bay Puritans, although they had not separated from the Church of England as the Pilgrims had, had been influenced by Deacon Fuller's description of Plymouth's more liberal congregational church services. They had also patterned their own form of government after the successful town meetings established by the Pilgrims.

"Samuel Fuller did more for the Puritans than heal their bodies," Bradford agreed, "and out of this small beginning greater things may come."

10

Plymouth Mourning
for Her Children

Governor William Bradford warmed his hands at the fire-place. How quiet the house was for market day. Alice and he often found it quiet now that their older children had married and had homes of their own. She had taken their twelve-year-old daughter, Mercy, to meet friends who came in from the neighboring farms and villages on Thursdays to buy and sell and visit together. Many of the people stayed for the midweek worship service. He hoped Alice would bring some of their old friends home to supper.

Why did he feel so tired? He was not quite fifty years old, but every year had brought more complicated problems than the last. He had been right about the Bay Colony. These godly men could be so exasperating doing only what they believed to be right!

In the past nine or ten years, men from Massachusetts Bay had set up trading posts near those of Plymouth's in Connecticut at Windsor. Bradford had written a sharp letter to Winthrop saying that Plymouth had braved the dangers of far settlements alone, had bought land from the Indians for their posts, and would not be crowded out now.

As Massachusetts Bay grew, its settlers had moved out farther and farther and had finally begun to build homes on Plymouth's territory. The Pilgrims who had moved out from Plymouth were in almost constant dispute with Bay settlers over boundary lines.

Although the two colonies were on reasonably neighborly terms, Bradford was often in contest with the Bay to keep the big colony from absorbing Plymouth.

He was equal to the battle with the Bay, he thought. Something much more serious troubled him now, the movement of his own people away from Plymouth.

When Plymouth began to prosper, the Pilgrims could afford more land and cattle and larger homes. Families moved where land could be had. Edward Winslow had built a house at Marshfield. The Standish and Alden families lived in Duxbury. Even Elder Brewster, after his wife died, had gone to Duxbury to live with one of his sons there.

Bradford hated to see Plymouth lose any part of its family, but these old friends were nearby and visited back and forth often, attended services, and voted in Plymouth. Now there was a group of young men and their wives and families who wanted to move in a body to Nauset (Eastham) on Cape Cod.

The governor had been aware of the discontent growing among some of the people, particularly the young newcomers who had not endured the hardships of settling Plymouth. He had taken the problem before the council and was astonished to learn that most of its members were embarrassed by their loyalty to him, their friend and governor, and that their sympathy was for the hopes of their own children.

"My son, Giles, is among those who want to go to Cape Cod," Stephen Hopkins said, "and my son-in-law, Nicholas Snow."

"My son-in-law, Thomas Prence, wants to go," Elder Brewster had said. "He has been trying to convince me that my grandchildren will have a better future at Nauset. He says there is not enough land near Plymouth to satisfy their needs."

"Of course they know that none of them can go to Nauset," Edward Winslow said, "unless you grant them the land, for you possess everything in your name, Will."

"I will not!" Governor Bradford had been so disturbed that he stood up and left his place at the head of the table. Then he turned and went back to his friends.

"I hold none of Plymouth Plantation's lands for myself," he said. "I have bought or traded for my own land as any other man. Yet I refuse to give up my privilege to hold the lands in my name. If Plymouth's land could be bought and sold by anyone, our community, so tightly bound together by love and brotherhood, would be destroyed."

"Will is right," Miles Standish said.

Finally Brewster had said, "We are between two fires, Will. You must decide this for yourself."

He had decided, William Bradford thought, walking back and forth in front of the fireplace, waiting for Alice to come home. Last night a messenger had brought him a verbal petition from the restless young families. They demanded to know why no more land had been granted outright to families after the patent had been taken in Bradford's name. The governor had answered by sending out a message today summoning all the men of the colony to assemble at the Fort for a Court of the People, at nine o'clock in the morning on Tuesday next.

"I must make them understand how wrong this is for them," he said aloud now.

"What's wrong?" Alice asked, taking off her bonnet.

He had not heard her come home and he felt a little foolish to be discovered talking to himself. He saw that she was distressed by the tension, hurt, and anger that must show in his face.

"No one came to supper with us," he said. "Are they talking on the street about the meeting on Tuesday? Do they know what I am going to say?"

She came and touched his arm. "Dear, dear Will," she said. "They do not mean to be critical. Remember how stubbornly you clung to what you wanted to do when you were young?"

"I refuse them for their own good," he said. "These young men would lose everything our sacrifice has gained for them."

"Oh, Will," she said, "you sound exactly like your Uncle Robert."

He was shaken by her words and went over and stood by the

table where he had sat late so many nights for so many years, making plans for the survival of his beloved Plymouth.

Could he have grown set in his ways and fearful of change as his uncles had been? He had long ago forgiven them, but he had never really known how they felt until now. His uncles had feared for him as he feared for Plymouth. Yet he had gone.

It is not the same, he told himself. He had gone for conscience' sake. These young men wanted only to prosper.

Yet, he thought, he had taken his choice and left home and later became a governor. Is that what these young men ask of me? Their own choice? He shook his head. They were too inexperienced to understand the risk to their very salvation if they left this well-ordered community.

He turned to the fireplace and looked into the flames. He heard Alice go into the kitchen and begin to prepare supper. He bent his head, "Give me wisdom, Lord."

Tuesday morning Governor Bradford, wearing his magistrate's long robe, walked up the hill to the Fort. He entered the low-ceilinged room lighted by narrow slits made for defense rather than for light. About a hundred men were seated on the wood benches. As Bradford stepped upon the platform and sat down in the governor's armchair to face them, he felt their expectancy, their doubt, and resistance.

Then he saw Elder Brewster's white head, and the faithful Standish frowning as if to quell the critics. There was Edward Winslow and John Alden, and Stephen Hopkins looking distressed by his divided loyalty. They had come knowing how their governor felt and they would back him no matter what he said.

Elder Brewster opened the meeting with prayer. He asked God to guide their thoughts, to help them understand and love one another, and in particular to be with their governor in his difficult decision.

There was a restless movement among the men when Brewster sat down. Everyone loved the gentle old man, but all knew he was on Bradford's side.

Governor Bradford stood. He had grown more calm during the prayer. He had never felt stronger, taller, more sure of himself as he began to speak.

He told of the fervor and devotion of the small group of Separatists at Scrooby who had risked their lives and fortunes to escape to Holland for religious freedom. As one family they had helped one another on the journey and then for twelve years in Leyden. Together they had endured the voyage of the *Mayflower*, the terrible sickness and deaths of half their people. The remaining half had lived only because of the loving attention and nursing of the sick by those who could stay on their feet. Yes, the Pilgrims had learned early of the need men had for one another.

The room was hushed now. Even those young men whom Bradford had had to place in stocks for punishment, and who might have come here hoping to see his authority overthrown, were quiet and listening. For the governor was a master of drama when he chose.

He reminded them of what this Fort and cluster of houses had cost them and of the years of hunger. They had survived by sharing everything, a community banded together to help one another. This way of life, this beloved community, was the thing he did not want to lose now, as much for them as for himself.

He saw that many men were moved, others stubborn. His voice grew stern.

Plymouth was prosperous, yet still in debt. The men had been willing enough, he reminded them, to leave their debts to the Undertakers, who were still struggling to pay them. The Undertakers had also spent a large sum of their own money in England to obtain the right to the land in the company's patent. Land held in Bradford's name, with his the privilege to lease or hold it.

He paused, then suddenly, with no warning of the change of mind that had come as he stood before the fireplace on market-day night remembering his own youth, he made his offer.

"I have decided to surrender the patent taken out in my name," he said.

He saw surprise and shock on the upturned faces of the men before him, and he continued. "I have never wanted wealth or power for myself. I have worked only for the good way of life we knew in Scrooby and again in this community. We have lived as a family, with warmth and love toward one another, tempered with discipline. Here, good men and women have been bound together by a purpose that gave us vision and courage for our lives. For almost twenty years we have enjoyed this life of close association at Plymouth. I cannot force any of you to continue it.

"That you may each choose freely for yourself, I give to the freemen of this corporation of New Plymouth all the privileges, immunities, and other benefits of the patent. I ask only that the oldcomers be granted the right to first choice of lands for themselves and their heirs, for they have endured much and received little of material things.

"Secondly, I ask that you agree to pay to me and my Undertaker partners up to 300 pounds if we are forced to sell any of our own land to repay the debt to the London Adventurers. For all that we have borrowed and spent over the years has been for the benefit of all."

In minutes the men voted to accept Bradford's overwhelmingly generous offer. One by one they spoke with respect to the governor as they left the Fort. Brewster was the last to shake his hand but even he did not stay to talk.

William Bradford walked home to tell Alice what he had done. He knew he had won a battle with himself and he had won the men again at this meeting. But his triumph was mixed with sorrow, for some of the people would go. Many of the younger families would move away to make their homes where there was more land.

Plymouth and our poor church will be left, he thought, like an ancient mother grown old and forsaken by her children.

Yet many friends would remain. He would stay with them, working as always for the good of Plymouth colony.

Afterwards

William Bradford was governor of Plymouth from the age of thirty-one to age sixty-seven, except for five different years when he pleaded for a rest and time to manage his own increasing lands and business. Even during these five years, he was elected assistant to Allerton or Prence. And he found that no matter who sat in the governor's chair, the people brought their problems to him, Bradford. At last he gave up and accepted the responsibility of governor until he died.

All Plymouth mourned that seventh day of May, 1657, when William Bradford lay seriously ill. His wife and many young men reared in his home took turns sitting beside him and telling him the news of the colony.

His faith was strong that he would see his Maker and the old friends who had died before him: Brewster, Winslow, and Standish. "God has given me a pledge of my happiness in another world," he told Alice.

The next evening at nine o'clock, he died. Neighboring colonies sent messages of sympathy to Plymouth. One from Massachusetts Bay stated that Bradford was mourned by "all the colonies of New England as a common blessing and father to them all."

Governor Bradford was buried on the hill overlooking the town he loved. Every man, woman, and child in Plymouth, and from miles around, was at the brief service. A prayer was said and a volley of shot fired over his grave.

Today, more than three hundred years later, a marble shaft stands on the hill engraved with this reminder: "Do not basely relinquish what the Fathers with difficulty attained."

The Author Says

There are no portraits of any of the Pilgrims (except one of Edward Winslow done in England when he was older), but Governor William Bradford left vivid word pictures of the small group of men, women, and children who settled at Plymouth, and whose ideas still influence the lives of everyone in the United States today.

Bradford's handwritten history, a journal or diary, with pages bound together like a book, was handed down in his family from father to son. During the first hundred years, it was loaned from time to time to learned men who were writing histories of early America or of the church. Then when the Revolutionary War began, the journal disappeared. For years it could not be found.

Did the Tory Governor Hutchinson of Massachusetts, who had once borrowed it, take Bradford's manuscript to England when he fled? Or was it stolen from Old South Church in Boston when many books were taken by British soldiers?

Until 1855 the manuscript was believed to have been destroyed with all its history of the early Pilgrim years. Then someone, leafing through a book published in England, came upon a reference to Bradford's journal. Greatly excited, the reader called this reference to the attention of American historians, who finally traced the source. Bradford's lost manuscript was found in the library of the Bishop of London, who did not know how it got there.

Immediately Massachusetts appealed to England for return of the stolen manuscript. It was more than forty-five years and after many appeals by state and federal officials and American historical societies before England finally gave up Bradford's history to the State of Massachusetts in 1897.

William Bradford's clear careful handwriting, today more than three hundred years old, was placed in a glass case of the State Library in the Boston State House. Here, in the record of *what he did* as leader of the Pilgrims, is the true picture.

I first read Bradford's *Of Plimoth Plantation* under the title *Log of the Mayflower* (Houghton, 1901), when I was researching for two of my books for young children, *Pilgrim Thanksgiving* and *Christmas on the Mayflower* (Coward-McCann).

Since then a complete text has been published in modern spelling.* I highly recommend it and the other following titles:

Benét, Stephen Vincent, *Western Star*. Henry Holt & Co., Inc., 1943. A history in poetry of the Pilgrims and the Virginia colony.

* Bradford, William, *Of Plymouth Plantation: 1620–1647*, intro. and notes by Samuel Eliot Morison. Alfred A. Knopf, Inc., 1952.

Mort's Relations. A journal of Bradford's and Winslow's letters, records, and writings, first published in London, 1622.

Smith, Bradford, *Bradford of Plymouth*. J. B. Lippincott Company, 1951.

Willison, George, *Saints and Strangers*. Reynal & Hitchcock, 1945.

Willison, George, ed., *The Pilgrim Reader*. Doubleday & Company, Inc., 1953.

W.P.H.

Author's Biography

Wilma Pitchford Hays has written thirty books, fiction and nonfiction, for children of all ages, many of them with authentic historical backgrounds. Born in Nebraska, she began at an early age to "make up" stories for her younger brother and four sisters. Later she told stories to her daughter, and now to her three grandchildren, all under three years of age, who live in Branford, Connecticut.

Mrs. Hays has worked with children all her life. She was a teacher before she married a superintendent of schools. Their daughter became a supervisor of music in public schools. When she sang in the musical *The Sound of Music*, she helped to coach the children in that show during a year's tour across the United States.

Mrs. Hays says, "I began writing for adults, but found children such wonderfully appreciative readers that I continued writing for them after publication of my first children's book, *Pilgrim Thanksgiving*, in 1955."

Mrs. Hays and her husband summer in New England but have moved to Venice, Florida, where she writes and also enjoys walking on the Gulf beaches to pick up shells and fossils.

In recent years Plymouth Plantation has been restored to its former appearance. When you visit it, Mrs. Hays suggests that you go on to Cape Cod (which was her home for some years) and see dunes and shoreline much as they were when the Pilgrims first set foot in this new world. Walk up Cornhill (Truro) where the Pilgrims found their first seed corn. Bathe at First Encounter Beach where the men met the Indians in a brief skirmish. Visit the graves of Giles Hopkins and two other passengers from the *Mayflower,* who were among those Pilgrims who demanded of Bradford the right to leave Plymouth and settle on Cape Cod at Eastham. When you visit some of the historical places there, you may be reminded of the Pilgrims.

Index

Adventurers: contract made with Separatists, 34–35, 52; failure of communal system for colony, 69; relations with colony, 56–58, 64, 66, 74, 76, 77, 88. *See also* Weston, Thomas

Alden, John, 38, 50, 53, 77, 84, 86

Allerton, Isaac, 34, 35, 49, 54, 56, 59, 74, 76, 77, 78, 89

Amsterdam, 20, 26–28

Ancient Brethren, 26

Anglican Church, 12, 16, 19, 33

Anne, 71–73

Billington: boys, John and Francis, 50–51; John, father, 80

Boston (England), 21–22

Boston (Mass.), 80, 90

Bradford, William: on Cape Cod, 39–43, 67–69; childhood, 1–20; family, 12–13, 16, 28, 41, 58, 71–75, 83–86; first chosen governor, 49; flees England, 21–25; in Holland, 26–36; journal, *Of Plimoth Plantation*, 56, 70, 91–92; marries Dorothy May, 28; marries Alice Southworth, 73; in Plymouth, 44–90; surrenders patent, 87–88; terms as governor, 89

Brewster, Elder William, 11, 12, 14, 19, 20, 23–24, 27, 29, 31, 33, 35, 38, 39, 42, 49–50, 56, 61, 65, 66, 72, 77, 81, 84, 86, 89

Carver, John, 32, 35, 40, 44, 46, 48, 49

Charity, 65–66, 71

Charleston, 78, 79

Chatham, 39, 67

Christmas, Pilgrims' first and second, 61

Clark, John, 38, 44

Clyfton, Pastor, 12, 22

Cornhill, 42–43, 49, 51

Court of High Commission, 14

Cushman, Robert, 32, 34, 35, 56–57

Discovery, 67

Dotey, Edward, 53–54

Dutch New Netherlands Company, 34

Duxbury, 84

Eastham (Nauset on Cape Cod), 43, 69, 84

Eaton, Francis, 53

Endicott, Governor John, 78, 80, 81

Fortune, 57, 58, 59, 61, 64, 66

Fuller, Samuel, 29, 34, 35, 50, 56, 78, 81

Gorges, Sir Ferdinando, 78

Great North Road, 11, 13, 16, 17

Green Gate meetinghouse, 28, 31, 32, 36

Hampton Court Conference, 17

Hobomok, 53, 59, 60, 62, 63

Holland and the Separatists: in Amsterdam, 26–27; haven for dissenters, 20; in Leyden, 27–36; reasons for leaving, 30; Scrooby Separatists emigrate, 22–25

Hopkins, Constance, 54

Hopkins, Giles, 84

Hopkins, Stephen, 38, 40, 42, 50, 53, 54, 56, 84, 86

Huddleston, Captain John, 65

Indian tribes: Massachusetts, 54, Narraganset, 59–60, 63; Nauset, 49, 51; Pawtuxet, 47; Wampanoag, 48, 52

Indians, 41–43; first encounters with, 44, 46–47, 51. *See also* Hobomok, Indian tribes, Massasoit, Samoset, Squanto

Jones, Captain, 35, 37–39, 43, 47, 61

King James, 17, 19–20, 33

Leister, Edward, 53–54
Leyden, 27–30, 33, 55, 87
Lion, 79

Maine, 64, 65; Monhegan Island, 74
Marshfield, 84
Massachusetts Bay, 54, 62, 65, 78
Massachusetts Bay Colony (the Bay), 78–80, 82, 83–84, 89
Massasoit, Chief, 48, 49, 51–55, 62, 63, 73
May, Dorothy, 27; became Dorothy Bradford, 28, 33, 36, 41, 45
Mayflower, 37, 45, 47, 50
Mayflower Compact, 40
Meetinghouse-Fort, 71, 73, 77, 81, 85–87
Morton, Nathaniel, 75
Mullins, Priscilla, 50

New England, 31, 33, 41, 89

Perth Assembly, 32
Pilgrims, origin of name for Separatists, 31–32
Plymouth: Pilgrims' first sight of, 44–45; Plymouth colony, 46–90
Plymouth Plantation's royal patent, 78, 79, 85, 87
Prence, Thomas, 77, 84, 89
Provincetown, 39
Purchasers, the, 77
Puritans, 11, 16–18, 78–79; differ from Separatists, 12

Queen Elizabeth, 12, 14, 15, 17, 38

Robinson, Pastor John, 18, 21, 22, 28, 32, 33, 36

Saltonstall, Sir Richard, 80
Samoset, 47

Scrooby, 11–14, 19, 22, 87
Separatists: as viewed by Bradford's family, 16, 19; as viewed by English government, 15, 17–18, 19, 20; become Pilgrims, 31–32; differ from Puritans, 12; early beginnings, 11–18
Smith, Captain John, 31, 33, 41, 44
Snow, Nicholas, 84
Southampton, 35–36
Southworth, Alice, 71–72; became Alice Bradford, 73, 79, 81, 85
Spaniards and their attack on Leyden, 29–30, 55
Speedwell, 36, 37
Squanto, 46–49, 51, 53, 59, 60, 62–64, 68
Standish, Captain Miles, 38, 41, 44, 46, 48, 50, 54, 56, 60, 66, 76, 77, 84, 85, 89
Strangers, the, 35, 38, 40
Swan, 65, 67, 68

Thanksgiving: first in Plymouth, 55–56; observed by Dutch in Leyden, 30
Truro, 39

Undertakers, the, 77, 87, 88

Virginia colony, 31, 33, 65, 67
Virginia Company, 32–34

Warwick, Earl of, 78
Weston, Thomas, 34, 35, 38, 50, 52, 59, 61, 64–67. *See also* Adventurers
White: family, 29; Mrs. Susan, 53
Williams, Roger, 81–82
Windsor, 83
Winslow, Edward, 29–31, 33–35, 48, 50, 53, 56, 65, 66, 73, 77, 86, 89, 91
Winthrop, Governor John, 78–82, 83

Yarmouth, 68
Yorkshire, 11, 12